Contents

HTML

MIKE McGRATH

In easy steps is an imprint of Computer Step
Southfield Road . Southam
Warwickshire CV47 0FB . England

http://www.ineasysteps.com

Notice of Liability

Every effort has been made to ensure that this book contains accurate and current information. However, Computer Step and the author shall not be liable for any loss or damage suffered by readers as a result of any information contained herein.

Trademarks

All trademarks are acknowledged as belonging to their respective companies.

Printed and bound in the United Kingdom

ISBN 1-84078-254-4

Introducing HTML

Welcome to the world of HyperText Markup Language (HTML) – the popular standard for the creation of Internet pages.

This chapter introduces HTML with a brief history and examines how HTML fits into the World Wide Web. There is a discussion of authoring tools and a demonstration of Web page structure.

Covers

Chapter One

History of HTML

Historically, the desire to have text printed in specific formats meant that original manuscripts had to be "marked up" with annotation to indicate to the book-printer how sections of text should be laid out.

W3C is the recognized body that oversees standards on the Web. See the latest developments on their informative Web site at *www.w3c.org*.

This annotation had to be concise and needed to be understood both by the printer and the text originator.

A series of commonly recognized abbreviations therefore formed the basis of a markup language.

HTML is a modern markup language that uses common abbreviations called "tags" to advise a Web browser how the author would like to have the Web page displayed.

It was devised in the late 1980s by a British scientist named Tim Berners-Lee while he was working at the Particle Physics laboratory in Cern, Switzerland.

The simplicity of HTML led it to become popular in the early days of the Internet with text-based Web browsers.

A major development with HTML came in 1993 when a college student named Marc Andreessen added an image tag so that HTML could display images in addition to text.

This version was then included in the Mosaic Web browser from the National Center for Supercomputing Applications (NCSA) and became very successful.

The current version of Microsoft Internet Explorer is based on the Mosaic browser from NCSA.

Marc went on to establish the Netscape Web browser.

By the mid 1990s various Web browsers that were fighting for market share began to add proprietary tags to effectively create their own versions of HTML.

The World Wide Web Consortium (W3C) recognized the danger that HTML could become fragmented and acted to create a standard to which all Web browsers should adhere. Today Tim Berners-Lee is a director of the W3C.

The latest recommended version of the W3C HTML standard is HTML 4.01. This version is covered throughout the book, but is generically referred to as HTML 4 or just HTML.

What's new in HTML 4

The features in the earlier standard of HTML 3.2 are updated in HTML 4 to provide more flexibility for current and future development of the Internet.

The style sheet examples given in this book use specifications of version CSS2.0.

HTML 4 separates the presentational markup tags from the actual content with the introduction of Cascading Style Sheets (CSS) that are used to control how content appears.

This is the single biggest change in HTML 4 but there are many other significant changes.

All tags are still contained between the **<** and **>** angled brackets but many of the earlier tags have become obsolete.

The old **<center>** tag is no longer used to center text on the page nor is the **<font>** tag now used to control the selection of a font style for a piece of text.

Instead a "stylesheet" controls these presentational details.

The range of available stylesheet properties gives much greater possibilities in how the content may be displayed.

New tags have been added to extend the precision of how HTML may define the document content.

To increase the global utilization of HTML, support has been added for languages that are written from right to left.

A new model is introduced for the layout of tables that allows a browser to start rendering a table even before the entire table has been downloaded.

Greater scripting possibilities have been created by the addition of more page "events" that react to the user.

HTML 4 has been designed to make Web pages more accessible to those with physical limitations.

Exciting possibilities are presented with the inclusion of further new tags for the creation of compound Web documents. These allow multiple documents from a variety of sources to be combined into a single Web page.

Addressing web pages

The really special component of HTML is the hypertext link that allows the user to easily navigate around the Internet.

In order for this to be possible the Internet must use established standards for all computers which are connected to the World Wide Web.

The Web comprises a series of large computers, referred to as 'servers', that are connected via telephone and satellite. Connecting any computer by telephone to any one of these servers can provide access to all files across the Web.

The Web uses a common communication standard called HyperText Transfer Protocol (HTTP) to allow instant communication between all computers and Web servers.

This common protocol permits the Web browser to retrieve Web pages from any part of the Web and is always used as the first part of a Web page address, expressed as **http://**.

It is necessary for each Web document to have a unique address so that the user can locate a specific document. In the same way that a postal address may be a combination of city name, street name and addressee name, a Web address combines protocol name, domain name and file name.

HTML files are merely text files that have been saved with a file extension of either **.htm** or **.html** so a typical index Web page could have a file name of 'index.html'.

A Web page address should not contain any spaces.

If this page was uploaded to a Web server having the domain name 'www.webserver' then the page would be accessible across the Web using the Web page address of **http://www.webserver/index.html**.

Usually, uploaded files are placed in a folder on the server so its Web page address would include the folder name:

Protocol	Domain Name	File Name
http://	www.webserver/subfolder/	index.html

Absolute and relative addresses

The full address of a Web page, using the protocol, domain and file name, is called the 'absolute' address.

Below is an illustration of a folder on a Web server that has the domain name **www.webserver**.

The index Web page can be addressed with its absolute address of **http://www.webserver/webpages/index.html**.

If in doubt always use the full absolute address to avoid confusion.

HTML code in the **index.html** file can also address any files within the **webpages** folder just using their file name.

This is called the 'relative' address.

In the illustration, code in the **index.html** file can refer to the **next.html** file simply as **next.html**, or with the absolute address of **http://www.webserver/webpages/next.html**.

A relative address can also refer to a file within the upper level folder that contains the current folder by preceding its file name with the syntax ' ../ '.

In the illustration, any document in the **extra** folder could address the **next.html** document in the **webpages** folder as **../next.html**.

Alternatively the absolute address can also be used to address the **next.html** document from within any other document as **http://www.webserver/webpages/next.html**.

Fragment addresses

Navigating to either an absolute or relative address will normally open that document at the start of the page.

It is possible however to add navigation points to the HTML code inside a Web page to allow quick navigation to specific points in that page.

See chapter 7 on Hyperlinks And Anchors for more info and examples. These navigation points are called "anchors" and are always given a name by which they can be addressed.

In the example on the previous page the file named **next.html** has fragment anchors at the start, middle and end of the document.

These anchors are named **"top"**, **"middle"** and **"bottom"**.

This page can be opened in a Web browser at a specific point in the document by adding the required anchor name to the end of the page address.

These added anchor names are referred to as "fragment identifiers" and must be preceded by a **#** character.

The address to open **next.html** at the middle anchor is **http://www.webserver/webpages/next.html#middle**.

If addressing this page and anchor from another file in the same folder the relative address **next.html#middle** could be used to open the document at the middle anchor.

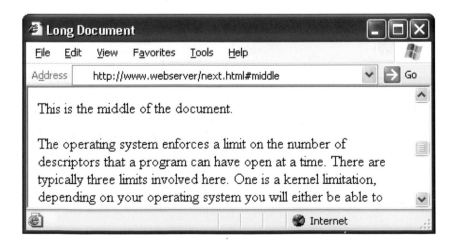

Document type definitions

The first line of each valid HTML document must contain a declaration of the version of HTML used in that document. This declaration is called a "Document Type Definition", or commonly just "DTD" for short.

The DTD is just a piece of code, specified in the HTML standard, that can be pasted into the top of each page.

The Web browser can use the address in the DTD to validate the HTML code contained in that document.

It states the Web page address containing the language rules for that version of HTML. The standard DTD is called "Strict" and should be used for a HTML document that only uses valid HTML 4 markup. For instance, the DTD using HTML version 4.01 looks like this:

```
<!DOCTYPE HTML PUBLIC "-//W3C//DTD HTML 4.01//EN"
         "http://www.w3.org/TR/html4/strict.dtd">
```

The specification also provides a "Transitional" DTD for backwards compatibility. This should be used where the HTML document contains some older markup that has become obsolete in the HTML 4 strict standard:

```
<!DOCTYPE HTML PUBLIC
         "-//W3C//DTD HTML 4.01 Transitional//EN"
         "http://www.w3.org/TR/html4/loose.dtd">
```

Finally there is a special DTD that is only to be used for a HTML "frameset" document that specifies the frames to be used in a multi-document Web page:

```
<!DOCTYPE HTML PUBLIC
         "-//W3C//DTD HTML 4.01 Frameset//EN"
         "http://www.w3.org/TR/html4/frameset.dtd">
```

Remember to add the appropriate DTD to the start of each HTML document so it may be validated.

As the example code given in this book does not use any obsolete markup the Strict DTD is used in all HTML documents except the frameset examples in chapter 9. The DTDs are not listed in any of the code samples in order to save space, but remember that they must be included at the start of each HTML document so they can be validated.

HTML document structure

A HTML 4 document comprises these three parts:

1. A Document Type Definition (DTD).

2. A Head section containing document information.

3. A Body section containing the actual content.

The DTD should appear at the top of the document to declare the HTML version being used in the document.

Develop the habit now of using lowercase characters for all HTML tags.

This is followed by a HTML **\<head\>** tag denoting the start of the Head section and a **\</head\>** tag to mark its end.

HTML tags are mostly used in this way as 'containers' with the syntax **\< tag name \> \</ tag name \>**.

The HTML **\<head\> \</head\>** tags contain the Head section information of a HTML document.

Similarly the HTML **\<body\> \</body\>** tags are used to contain the actual content of the HTML document.

The example below illustrates the three parts that comprise all HTML 4 documents:

Any text that appears between the special comment identifiers \<!--
and --> *is ignored by the browser.*

```
<!DOCTYPE HTML PUBLIC "-//W3C//DTD HTML 4.01//EN"
          "http://www.w3.org/TR/html4/strict.dtd">

<head>
<!-- The document information code goes here -->
</head>

<body>
<!-- The actual document content goes here -->
</body>
```

The HTML 4 tag names may use uppercase or lowercase characters. Future versions may allow only lowercase however so lowercase is used throughout this book.

Hello World

The head section of a document should always contain exactly one set of **<title>** tags. These are used to set the document title that is usually seen in the window title bar.

The example below adds a title in the head section and simple text inside **<p>** paragraph tags in the body section:

hello.html

```
<head>
<title>Greetings</title>
</head>

<body>
<!-- The Traditional Start -->
<p>Hello World</p>
</body>
```

 The old <html> tags that were used to enclose all the HTML code are no longer required to be used.

 The "invisible" characters that represent tabs, newlines, carriage returns and spaces are collectively known as "whitespace".

Notice that the code in the body section also contains a HTML comment that is not displayed by the browser.

This applies both to single-line comments and comments that are spread over many lines.

The Web browser also ignores the "invisible characters" that represent tabs, new lines, and carriage returns.

Multiple spaces are commuted to just a single space. This means that the browser output in the example above would remain the same even if the code left multiple spaces between the two content words.

HTML tools

HTML code can be created in any basic text editor and does not require any special software.

In fact, many professional HTML writers use the simple Notepad application included with Microsoft Windows.

As long as the code in the new text file is saved with a file extension of either ".htm" or ".html" a HTML file is made.

This file can then be opened in any recent version of Microsoft Internet Explorer to see the browser output.

Some Netscape browsers and other older browsers may not fully recognize the HTML 4 specifications.

It is best therefore to run HTML 4 Web pages in a modern version of Internet Explorer. This browser is also by far the most popular Web browser used on the Internet.

To validate the HTML code written in a finished document it is best to avoid the proprietary validator applications that are available which may not fully meet the standards.

Remember that all HTML 4 pages must begin with an appropriate DTD declaration – as described on page 13.

The W3C have a free on-line validation service that will quickly validate the code of any HTML 4 document.

If the HTML document is located on the Web the W3C HTML validator at **http://validator.w3.org** can be used for an instant validation.

If the document is just on the local computer, say on the desktop, use **http://validator.w3.org/file-upload.html** where the W3C validator will quickly upload the file then return instant validation results.

The validator has useful options and gives helpful output.

To encourage correct HTML code to be used on the Internet the W3C validator offers a verification image for correct validation results.

This can prove useful to Web developers to assure their clients that the code which they are supplying has been tested to the correct standards.

Microsoft FrontPage

The FrontPage application from Microsoft is one of the most successful of the so-called "WYSIWYG" HTML editors (What-You-See-Is-What-You-Get).

FrontPage and similar HTML editors can be used to create and quickly test handwritten HTML code.

They all offer the advantages of color highlighting of the HTML tags and other syntax when viewing the HTML code.

Also all have a quick and easy way to preview code under development that simulates its output in a Web browser.

FrontPage has tabs at the bottom of the window to toggle views between the code and preview windows.

 FrontPage does not make real validation checks on the HTML code and may appear to correctly preview bad code.

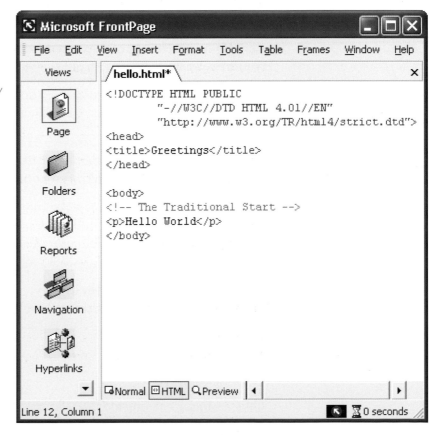

HTML authoring tips

The W3C make these general recommendations to Web page authors:

1. Separate structure and presentation

As the Internet develops, a wider range of devices are expected to access HTML documents on a variety of platforms (cellphones, PDAs, etc.).

It is therefore recommended that the Web page author should now use stylesheets for all presentational aspects of a HTML document.

This enables one document to be more easily readable across a wide range of devices and platforms. The process of making revisions to a HTML document is simplified and the cost of serving a wide range of platforms is reduced.

2. Consider universal accessibility

The Web page author is recommended to consider that their HTML documents may be accessed from a variety of special platforms by those users with physical limitations.

Many HTML 4 tags have attributes, such as **label**, that can be set to provide extra information for these users.

Also, with increasing globalization, a HTML document may be reaching a far-off audience that has different computer configurations to those of the originating computer.

Consequently, for documents to be interpreted correctly, the Web page author should include in their document information about the natural language used, direction of the text and how the document is encoded.

3. Speed-up table rendering

The table layout model in early versions of HTML often had to download the complete table data before the browser was able to render the table in the display.

Web page authors are recommended to make use of the table model in HTML 4 which has added features to help browsers render tables more quickly.

The document head

This chapter explores the head section of a HTML 4 page and illustrates by example how it can be used. The samples show how to describe features of the HTML document and how to add scripts and stylesheets to the page.

Covers

Chapter Two

Inside the head

The head section of a HTML document follows the obligatory Document Type Definition (DTD), as described on page 13, and is used to contain information about that document.

Typically this will include the document title and keywords that can be used by search engines to describe the document. The document head may also contain script code and stylesheets to determine how the contents should be presented.

For more about tag attributes see page 44.

In HTML 4 the entire head section may be contained within a pair of **\<head\> \</head\>** tags although these are entirely optional and only serve to group the head contents together.

When reading HTML code it does help to see the head section contents grouped by the **\<head\> \</head\>** tags so these are included in the examples given in this book.

More detail on meta data is given later in this chapter.

The **\<head\>** tag may optionally contain a new attribute named **profile** to specify the location of a "meta data" profile to be used by the document.

The **profile** attribute is not widely used but is given here for completeness and may appear in HTML code like this:

profile.html

```
<head profile =
        "http://www.purl.org/metadata/dublin_core">

    <!-- head section content goes here -->

</head>
```

Like many of the new features in HTML 4 the **profile** attribute has been included to accommodate possible future developments in the use of the language.

There are anticipated advances in the way that the HTML page may be viewed on a variety of browsers (user agents) such as cellphones, PDAs and other devices in addition to the traditional desktop PC web browser.

Document title

Each HTML 4 document must specify a document title.

There may be only one title and this should be contained within a pair of **<title> </title>** tags in the head section of the document.

 See page 62 for more on character entities.

The title may comprise both regular text characters and character entities for special characters such as ampersand, copyright mark and accented characters.

Although the document title is not part of the actual document content the HTML 4 specification states that the user-agent (browser) must always make the document title available to the user.

For this reason it is recommended that the given title should be as descriptive as possible to help describe the document.

For example, a document entitled "Intro" merely suggests that the document is an introduction to something.

Whereas a title of "An Introduction to HTML 4" describes the content and the topic of that document.

Traditional PC web browsers will display the document title in the title bar of the browser window as seen below:

```
<head>
<title>An Introduction to HTML 4</title>
</head>
```

title.html

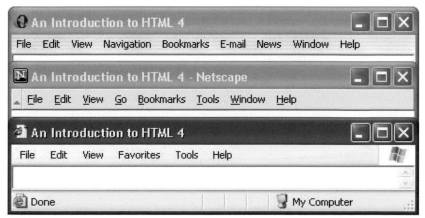

Meta information

Meta information is simply data that describes other data.

In the context of a HTML document meta data describes the document itself rather than the document content.

Meta data is defined in the head section of a document using the **<meta>** tag.

The **<meta>** tag is only used to declare data in its attributes so it does not have an associated closing tag.

The other possible attribute in the **<meta>** *tag is* **scheme** – *see an example on page 25.*

Most **<meta>** tags use the **content** and **http-equiv** attributes or the **content** and **name** attributes.

The **http-equiv** attribute can specify a data type to the server while the **content** attribute specifies the data itself.

For example, the **"Expires"** data type can be used to force a Web browser to download the latest version of a Web page.

Ordinarily a Web browser will load a cached copy of a Web page location if one is available in the browser's cache.

Using a **<meta>** tag the page can be set to expire so that the browser will seek the latest version from the server if the current date exceeds that specified by the **content** attribute.

The following example sets a page to expire at midnight on New Year's Eve 2004. It is important to specify the date in the exact format that is used in this example:

expires.html

```
<head>
<title>This Page Expires After 2004</title>
<meta http-equiv="Expires"
      content="Fri, 31 Dec 2004 23:59:59 GMT">
</head>
```

Assigning **"Refresh"** to the **http-equiv** attribute, to redirect users to another location, is not recommended because some browsers do not support this method. Instead a server-side script should be used to redirect browsers.

Character encoding

A **<meta>** tag can advise the browser of the character encoding used by the document content.

The **http-equiv** attribute is assigned as **"Content-type"** so the **content** attribute can then describe the document content.

Although not strictly a requirement of HTML it is recommended that all HTML document head sections should include meta data describing that document's character set.

The content should firstly be described as **"text/html;"** to tell the browser to expect to receive HTML content. Then the character encoding is specified as **"charset=** *character-set* **"**.

*HTML pages in the English language typically asssign the **charset** of "ISO-8859-1".*

There are literally dozens of character sets in use but the table below lists some of the most commonly found ones and the example specifies the **"Shift_JIS"** character encoding.

Name	Character Set
US-ASCII	US ASCII characters
ISO-8859-1	Standard ISO Latin-1 characters
UTF-8	Multi-lingual Universal Transformation Format
Shift_JIS	Japanese characters
Big5	Chinese traditional characters

charset.html

```
<head>
<title>Using SHIFT_JIS Encoding</title>
<meta http-equiv="Content-type"
      content="text/html; charset=Shift_JIS">
</head>
```

*Remember to include the semi-colon after the value **text/html**.*

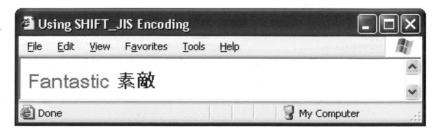

Search-engine meta data

Search engines are used by the main Internet portal sites, such as Yahoo, to return resulting links to documents containing keywords that have been entered by the user.

The methods used by the search engines vary and are constantly being updated to ensure variety of results.

Most search engines do however use, in part at least, the **<meta>** data provided in a document head section to return a link to that document for the user.

The two pieces of meta data sought by search engines are the document **"keywords"** and **"description"**. To make a document visible to search engines it is important to include both correctly.

The keywords should appear in a **<meta>** tag that uses a **name** attribute to specify the term **"keywords"**. The **content** attribute of this tag should be assigned a short list of relevant topical words that do actually appear in the page content, and listed preferably in the order in which they appear.

Use only lowercase characters for keywords as most users use these and some search engines are case-sensitive.

The description should appear in a **<meta>** tag that uses a **name** attribute to specify the term **"description"**. The **content** attribute of this tag should be assigned an accurate description of the document in less than 25 words.

In the following example the document head contains meta data to assist the search engine user who is seeking information for a wonderful Greek holiday:

metadata.html

```
<head>
<title>Greek Island Sunshine Holidays</title>
<meta name="keywords"
      content="Greek,Greece,holiday,sunshine">
<meta name="description"
      content="Idyllic Sunny Greek Holidays">
<meta http-equiv="Content-Type"
      content="text/html; charset=ISO-8859-1">
</head>
```

Custom meta data

More advanced use of meta data allows the document author to specify any custom properties of the document that may be useful to a browser.

For example, in a document describing this book it may be useful to add some of the relevant information as meta data:

metabook.html

```
<head>
<title>HTML in easy steps</title>
<meta name="author" content="Mike McGrath">
<meta name="ISBN" content="1-84078-254-4">
<meta http-equiv="Content-Type"
      content="text/html; charset=ISO-8859-1">
</head>
```

The examples given here illustrate some advanced uses of meta data.

This ability to add any custom values to the **<meta>** tag attributes will only be useful if they can be recognized. A major effort to consolidate meta data involves a profile standard named the "Dublin Core" that defines a set of recommended book properties. Current information about this profile together with full specifications can be found on the web at **http://purl.org/dc**.

The properties that are defined by a profile have their values set by subsequent **<meta>** tags within the document. The **<meta>** tag also has a **scheme** attribute that can be used in conjunction with a profile to help the browser correctly interpret the meta data.

In the example below a hypothetical profile defines a **scheme** to specify the format of an ISBN book number:

scheme.html

```
<head profile="http://acme.com/bookprofile">
<title>HTML in easy steps</title>
<meta scheme="ISBN" name="identifier"
      content="1-84078-254-4">
<meta http-equiv="Content-Type"
      content="text/html; charset=ISO-8859-1">
</head>
```

Adding scripts

Scripts enclosed by **<script> </script>** tags can be added to a document to interact with the user and provide dynamic content. It is convenient to locate scripts in the document's head section.

A **<script>** attribute called **type** should specify the scripting language to be used such as **"text/javascript"**. In order to avoid the script appearing as displayed text in older browsers that do not recognize the **<script>** tag the script block can start with **<!--** and end with **//-->** to hide the script.

Alternative content can be set outside the head with **<noscript> </noscript>** tags for browsers that do not recognize scripts:

script.html

It is incorrect to write complete HTML closing tags with JavaScript – technically the </ sequence, followed by any letter, is seen as the end tag for the <script> element. A workaround is to write the closing tag in separate parts, as shown here. This prevents the validator spotting an illegal closing tag in the head section so avoids validation failure.

```
<head>
<meta http-equiv="Content-Type"
      content="text/html; charset=ISO-8859-1">
<title>A Simple JavaScript Example</title>
<script type="text/javascript">
<!--
document.write("<p>Hello from JavaScript<");
document.write("/p>");
//-->
</script>
</head>

<noscript><p>Document uses JavaScript</p></noscript>
```

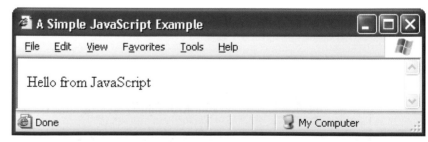

Scripts in remote files can be included with the **<script>** tag by adding a **src** attribute giving the location of the file:

```
<script type="text/javascript" src="myscript.js">
</script>
```

Adding stylesheets

Stylesheets can be added to a HTML 4 document head to influence how the document content is displayed. The stylesheet rules that define the content's appearance must be enclosed by **<style>** **</style>** tags. The stylesheet language must be specified by the **type** attribute of the **<style>** tag, such as "**text/css**".

In order to avoid the rules appearing as displayed text in those browsers that do not recognize the **<style>** tag the stylesheet can start with **<!--** and end with **//-->** to hide the stylesheet.

This example builds upon the previous one, adding a stylesheet to set the overall height of the text. It forces the first letter to be red and double the height of other text:

style.html

```
<head>
<meta http-equiv="Content-Type"
        content="text/html; charset=ISO-8859-1">
<title>A JavaScript Example With Style</title>
<style type="text/css">
<!--
p { font-size: 12pt; }
p:first-letter { font-size: 200%; color:red }
//-->
</style>
<script type="text/javascript">
<!--
document.write("<p>Hello from JavaScript<");
document.write("/p>");
//-->
</script>
</head>
```

This example is just to illustrate how to add a stylesheet to a document. Full examples of stylesheet rules are given later in this book.

Few old browsers that do not recognize <style> and <script> tags remain in use – so the <!-- --> hiding tags are not included in other examples in this book.

Linking resources

The **\<link\>** tag provides a means to link resources, such as an external stylesheet, to the document.

The value assigned to the **type** attribute must be a valid MIME type – see page 90 for more details on common MIME types.

This tag can only be used in the head section of a document but each head section can contain many **\<link\>** tags. Each of these are used to specify three attributes that define a resource type, location and relationship.

A **href** attribute specifies the location and a **type** attribute states the type of resource, such as **"text/html"**. A **rel** attribute specifies the relationship to the document as one of the following:

stylesheet	alternate	start	next	prev
contents	index	glossary	copyright	chapter
section	subsection	appendix	help	bookmark

The example below has a **\<link\>** tag to add an external stylesheet and another **\<link\>** tag to provide information of where a search engine can find the next page:

baselink.html

```
<head>
<meta http-equiv="Content-Type"
      content="text/html; charset=ISO-8859-1">
<title>The History Of The World - Page 1</title>
<base href="http://domain.com/docs/page1.html">
<link href="a.css" rel="stylesheet" type="text/css">
<link href="page2.html" rel="next" type="text/html">
</head>
```

Both **\<base\>** and **\<link\>** tags do not have closing tags.

Notice that the example uses a **\<base\>** tag to define the path to be used by subsequent pages. For this reason the **\<base\>** tag, if present, must be situated in the head section before mention of any other addresses.

The base path is by default that of the current document but using a **\<base\>** tag enables files located in the specified base directory to be addressed by just their file names.

Body text content

This chapter demonstrates how to incorporate text content into the body section of a HTML document. All the layout tags are described and examples of each one illustrate how they control the displayed text.

Covers

Chapter Three

The document body

Following the obligatory DTD and the head section code the document arrives at the document body where the actual content is written.

The code samples in this book do use the optional **<body>** *tags to enclose the page's body section.*

The HTML 4 specification does still have **<body> </body>** tags but these are now optional. Also the **<body>** attributes formerly used in HTML to specify background color, text color and hyperlink colors have all been made obsolete.

All of these colors should now be specified in a style sheet.

See chapter 4 for details on how to specify body colors in stylesheets.

The only two **<body>** attributes that remain fully valid in HTML 4 are **onload** and **onunload** that can be used to run script functions when the document loads and unloads.

This example illustrates the document **body** section and calls a JavaScript **alert()** function when the page loads and unloads:

load.html

```
<head>
<title>Using Load and Onunload</title>
</head>

<body onload="alert('Hi!')" onunload="alert('Bye')">

        <p><!-- document content goes here --></p>
</body>
```

Further code examples in this book usually omit the head section (and DTD) in order to save space on the page.

Content in paragraphs

Text content is traditionally separated into sentences and paragraphs to be more easily read and understood.

The basic tags that define the document text content into paragraphs are the **\<p> \</p>** tags.

These will visually separate the displayed text, normally leaving two empty lines between each paragraph.

Some browsers may ignore paragraphs that do not have a \</p> closing tag.

Although browsers may correctly render text into paragraphs without the closing **\</p>** tag its omission is bad practice and they are required to comply with the HTML Strict standard. The closing **\</p>** tag should always be included as shown in the example below and all examples throughout this book:

para.html

```
<body>

<p>In the midst of all its busy city life, Heraklion
has a number of interesting and endearing features.
</p>


<p>
One is the Venetian harbour - a good place to begin
a tour of the city.
</p>

</body>
```

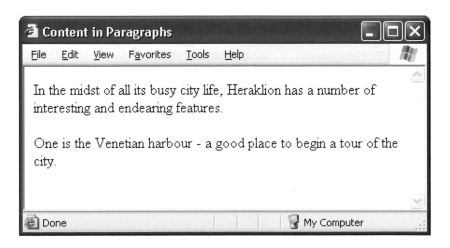

Forcing line breaks

When the body content is displayed text will, by default, wrap automatically to the next line after meeting the right-hand edge of the display area.

The browser will normally seek back in the text to find the last space at which to break the line.

This ensures that the line wraps intelligently so that the last whole word on the line is not broken.

A line break in the displayed text can be forced using the single **
** tag.

The **
** tag is always used without a closing tag.

This tag can be inserted as often as required and at any point in the text to force one or more line breaks.

In the following example the **
** tag is used to determine how the body text content should appear:

break.html

```
<body>
<p>
The top attraction in Heraklion is
<br>
the Venetian Castle,
<br>
still known by its Turkish name "Koúles".
</p>
</body>
```

Use the code **

** *to add a double line space between displayed text.*

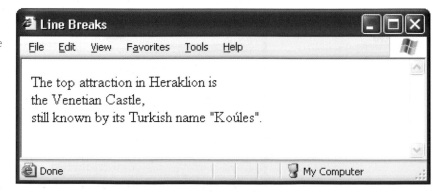

Quotes and blockquotes

In the HTML 4 specifications two tags are provided for the display of quotations within document body text content.

The **<q> </q>** quotation tags allow for short snippets of quoted text to be inserted into regular text content.

See page 62 for how to use quotation marks inside normal text.

Whereas the **<blockquote> </blockquote>** tags can be used to insert longer quotations into the body text.

Both of these tags accept a single attribute called **cite** that can be assigned an address indicating the quotation source.

Most browsers will render the **<blockquote>** content as an indented text as seen in the example below.

This indentation should not be used for presentational purposes though as not all browsers will act the same.

It is the intent of the HTML 4 specification that the browser should provide quote marks to surround content in each of these tags, although most may not fully comply.

quote.html

```
<body>
<p>Alexander spoke solemnly...</p>
<blockquote cite="http://domain.com/plutarch.html">
<p>If I were not Alexander, I would be Diogenes.</p>
</blockquote>
<p>according to Plutarch.</p>
</body>
```

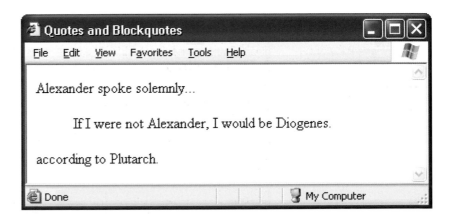

Headings

Headings in HTML documents are used to define sections of text in the same way as the heading on this page. There are six sets of heading tags available ranging from **<h1> </h1>** as the most important, down to **<h6> </h6>** as the least important.

Heading tags automatically add a line break to move onto the next line.

Browsers will generally display headings in increasingly larger fonts to emphasize their importance. In addition the browser could use the document headings to compile a list of topics that appear in that document.

The simple example below illustrates each of the headings as they appear when viewed in Microsoft Internet Explorer:

heading.html

```
<body>
<h1>H1 Heading</h1>
<h2>H2 Heading</h2>
<h3>H3 Heading</h3>
<h4>H4 Heading</h4>
<h5>H5 Heading</h5>
<h6>H6 Heading</h6>
</body>
```

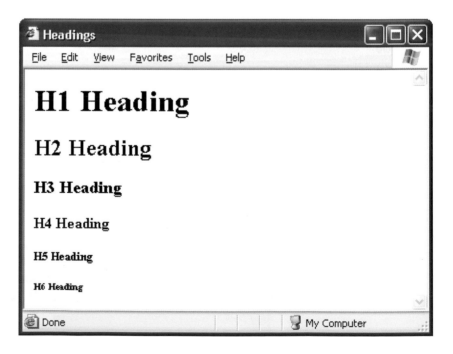

Emphasizing text

The text displayed in the body of a HTML document can be emphasized by making the font appear bolder, or in italic style, or in both bold and italic style.

To make the text bold requires the text to be contained inside a pair of **\<b> \</b>** tags. Alternatively, emphasis can be suggested using **\<strong> \</strong>** tags that will generally display the text in a bold font.

For italic text the **\<i> \</i>** tags must surround the text. Or emphasis can be suggested using **\<em> \</em>** tags that will generally display the text in an italic font.

Bold and italic text can be displayed by nesting one pair of tags inside the other as illustrated by this example:

emphasis.html

```
<body>
<p>This regular text can become<br> <b>bold</b> or
<i>italic</i> or <b> <i>bold italic</i> </b>
</p>
<p>This regular text can become<br>
<strong>strong</strong> or <em>em(phasized)</em> <br>
or <strong> <em>strongly emphasized</em> </strong>
</p>
</body>
```

Take care to close nested tags in the correct order to avoid errors –
\<b>\<i>text**\</b>\</i>**
is incorrect, whereas
\<b>\<i>text**\</i>\</b>**
is correct.

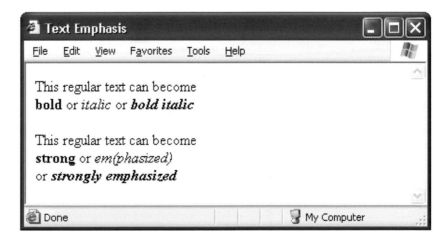

Text formatting

Text in the body of a HTML document will generally, by default, be displayed in the variable width font and font size selected by the user in the browser settings.

The **<tt> </tt>** tags can be used to force the browser to display text using the fixed width font selected by the user.

Font size can be varied using the **<big> </big>** tags to display text in a font size that is larger than the font that is used by default for regular text.

Use multiple **<big>** *or* **<small>** *tags for greater change away from the default font size.*

Also the **<small> </small>** tags may be used to display text in a font size that is smaller than that used for regular text.

The example below illustrates how text appearance can be formatted into fixed width font and a variety of font sizes:

format.html

```
<body>
<p>You can to see the high points of Heraklion
<br>
<tt>-the Archaeological Museum and Knossos-</tt>
<br>in a very <big>full</big> day.
<br>
<small><small>
But then you'd be missing the best of Crete.
</small></small>
</p>
</body>
```

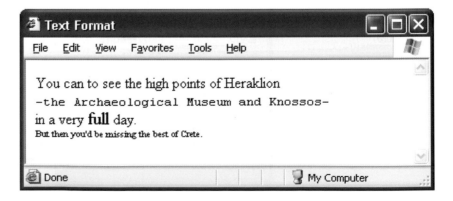

Preformatted text

The HTML **\<pre\>** tag is useful to retain the format characteristics of preformatted text within a document.

Any text within **\<pre\>** **\</pre\>** tags will be displayed to include the original spaces, tabs and line breaks that are collectively known as "whitespace".

The browser will not generally wrap preformatted text and may display the text in a fixed width font, as illustrated in the example listed below:

preform.html

The variable and fixed-width fonts are determined by the user's browser option settings.

```
<body>
<p>Greek signposts can confuse...</p>
<pre>
Chaniá

           Xaniá

                    Haniá

                         Khaniá
</pre>
<p>... all refer to the same town!</p>
</body>
```

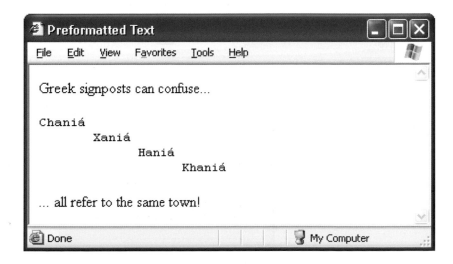

Subscript and superscript

The HTML **<sub>** and **<sup>** tags can be used to display text that is vertically altered from the regular text line.

For subscript text the **** tags display text shifted down by about half the line height of regular text.

Similarly the **** tags display superscript text shifted up by about half the line height of the regular text.

It should be noted that, although the position is shifted, the text is displayed normally in the same font throughout.

The subscript and superscript tags are especially useful for the display of some foreign language texts.

The example below illustrates both subscript and superscript displaying text with altered vertical alignment:

subsup.html

```
<body>
<p>
The chemical symbol H<sub>2</sub>O represents water.
<br>
In the West January 1<sup>st</sup> is New Years Day.
<br>
Surfers ride the w<sup>a</sup>v<sub>e</sub>s
on the ocean.
</p>
</body>
```

*The **<small>** tag could additionally be used to reduce the font for the "2" in the first line.*

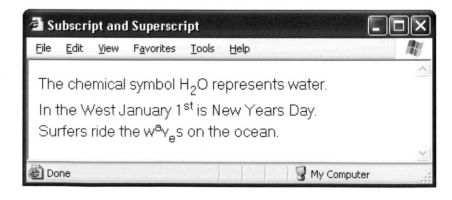

Contact address

The HTML **<address>** tag can be used to supply contact information regarding a document.

It may often be found at the start or end of a document providing a link to a page giving more information about the author of that document.

For more on hyperlinks see chapter 7.

It could also be used to provide information regarding the authorship of a particular form within a document.

In the example below the **<address>** tag incorporates a hyperlink to another page about the document's author:

address.html

```
<body>
<h3>Fun With HTML 4</h3>
<p>The latest specification of HTML is great.</p>
<address>
This article by:
<a href="mikem.html">Mike McGrath</a> <br>
Your comments are welcome.
</address>
</body>
```

With this example the browser has automatically chosen to display any text within the <address> tag in italic font.

Displaying code in text

HTML 4 specifications provide three tags for the specific purpose of describing pieces of computer programming code when it is to be displayed in a document.

The **\<code> \</code>** tags are used to denote that the text contained between the tags is indeed programming code.

Reference in the general document text to instances of a variable in the programming code may use **\<var> \</var>** tags to denote a program variable.

Any samples of text output from a program can be denoted in the document text by the **\<samp> \</samp>** tags.

The example below uses these tags to describe a simple JavaScript program in the general document text:

code.html

```
<body>
<p>When this simple JavaScript is run:</p>
<p>
<code>var content="Hello";<br>
document.write(content);</code>
</p>
<p>the <var>content</var>
is written as <samp>Hello</samp> on the page.
</p>
</body>
```

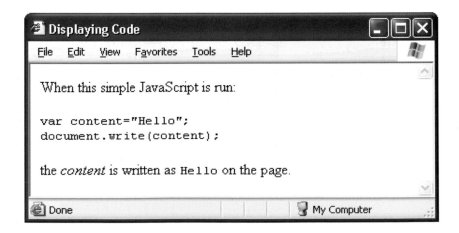

Advisory tags

The tags **<abbr> </abbr>** and **<acronym> </acronym>** can be used to denote abbreviations and acronyms.

These tags may be useful, for example, to exclude the tag contents from a spell checker.

The **<dfn> </dfn>** tags can be used to indicate the definitive meaning for a given term and **<cite> </cite>** tags may be used as a reference to another source.

Also **<kbd> </kbd>** tags indicate text that a user can input.

All of these tags are illustrated in the example below that assigns a meaningful value to the **title** attribute of each tag:

advise.html

```
<body>
<p>You can learn
<abbr title="Common Gateway Interface">CGI</abbr>
scripting with
<acronym title="Practical Enquiry and Reporting
Language">PERL</acronym> from <br>
<dfn title="PerlBook">"PERL in Easy Steps"</dfn>
by <cite title="Author">Mike McGrath</cite>
</p>
<p>Press <kbd title="agree">Y</kbd>
on your keyboard for more details.
</p>
</body>
```

Browsers choose how to use the given information – here Internet Explorer displays the title value as a "tooltip" when the cursor is over the text.

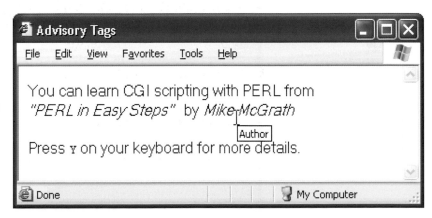

Delete and insert

There are two special tags that can be used to identify text that has been deleted or inserted in respect of an earlier version of that document.

This may be particularly appropriate when updating draft documents to reveal the changes.

The **\<del\> \</del\>** and **\<ins\> \</ins\>** tags used for this purpose are unusual as they can be applied in two ways.

Firstly the tags can be applied "in-line" to a word or several words in a paragraph as usual.

Also they can be used to contain entire paragraphs, lists and tables that have been changed.

This example uses these tags in-line to change "1" into "2" and then to change a complete paragraph:

dekins.html

```
<body>
<p>
The option permits <del>1</del> <ins>2</ins> selections.
</p>

<del> <p>This is the first draft content.</p> </del>

<ins> <p>This is the second draft content.</p> </ins>

</body>
```

The tags define the changed text but the browser will decide how to utilize this information.

Adding style to content

This chapter introduces tag attributes and the principles of stylesheets as a means to determine the presentation of content. Examples illustrate how HTML tags can define pieces of text content so that the stylesheet may specify how each piece of text should be displayed.

Covers

Chapter Four

About tag attributes

Attributes are features of the HTML specification that can be added inside individual tags to make them more useful.

To add an attribute to a tag requires that the attribute name is added inside the tag followed by "=" and a given value.

Tags that can be used in the document body to display content can accept any of the attributes listed in this table:

Tags used to provide information about the document have other attributes – see the examples in chapter 2.

Attribute	Specifies
id	document-wide unique id name for element
class	class name to apply associated style rules
style	simple in-line style rule
lang	language in short coded form
dir	direction of text either rtl or ltr
onclick	mouse click action
ondblclick	mouse double-click action
onmousedown	mouse button pressed action
onmouseup	mouse button released action
onmouseover	pointer moves on element action
onmouseout	pointer moves off element action
onmousemove	pointer moves within element action
onkeypress	key pressed and released action
onkeydown	key pressed action
onkeyup	key released action

These attributes cannot be used inside tags that are used to denote information about the document such as **<base>**, **<head>**, **<meta>**, **<param>**, **<style>** and **<script>**.

Using tag attributes

To use a tag attribute its name must be added inside the tag together with an assigned value enclosed within quotes.

In the table opposite all tag attributes that begin with "on" assign "event-handlers" that will perform an action each time a particular event occurs.

The event-handler will normally be a script function that will perform the desired action.

Always use a stylesheet to apply rules rather than the style attribute.

A piece of document text can have a style rule applied in-line with the **<style>** tag. It is better to use a stylesheet though to keep all the style rules together.

Multiple attributes can be added inside a single tag.

This example adds a **style** attribute to apply a style rule to the font and adds an **onclick** attribute that will open an alert dialog whenever the onclick event occurs:

attribs.html

```
<head>
<title>Using Tag Attributes</title>
</head>

<body>
<p style="font-family:cursive; color:red"
   onclick="alert('Mouse Clicked')">Click Here
</p>
</body>
```

A first stylesheet

Stylesheets are used in HTML 4 documents to influence how aspects of the document content should be displayed.

The code that determines how each part of the content should appear is referred to as the stylesheet "rules".

Stylesheet rules must be located in the stylesheet block that is situated in the **head** section of a HTML document.

The syntax of a stylesheet rule first states the part of the content to affect followed by a list of its attributes and values inside a pair of curly brackets **{ }**.

Attribute names must be recognized for the stated document part and the assigned value must be valid for that attribute.

Each attribute and its value are separated by a colon and each **attribute:value** pair is terminated with a semi-colon.

This example applies stylesheet rules to the document body itself to create a yellow-colored background with all text in red:

The trailing semi-colon can be omitted after the final **attribute:value** *pair, or if the rule specifies just one* **attribute:value** *pair.*

```
<head>
<title>Body Styling</title>
<style type="text/css">
body { background-color: yellow; color:red }
</style>
</head>

<body>
<p>This is a first style sheet.</p>
</body>
```

bodystyle.html

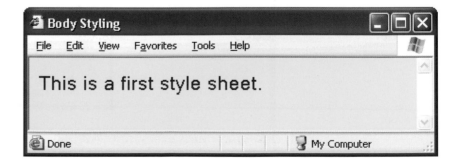

Styling tags

Style sheet rules can be applied to a selected tag so that each occurrence of that tag in the document content is affected.

This example changes the color and font for all **<h3>** content:

tagstyle.html

```
<head>
<title>Tag Styling</title>
<style type="text/css">
h3 { font-family:monospace; color:red }
</style>
</head>

<body>
<h2>Museums</h2>
<h3>Archaeological Museum</h3>
<p>The most important collection of Minoan art and
artifacts in the world.</p>
<h3>Historical Museum</h3>
<p>The history of Crete from Byzantine to modern times.
</p>
</body>
```

Notice how this example does not change the **<h2>** heading or the font used for any other text.

Stylesheets are more fully called Cascading Style Sheets after the way a style rule "cascades" through a document, applying presentational qualities to each instance of its specified element.

Styling with Class

All HTML 4 tags that are used to display content can accept an attribute called **class** to which a name can be assigned. The **class** name can be used in a stylesheet to apply rules so that any tag bearing that **class** name will apply its rules.

The example below defines a **class** named "myclass" with a rule to change content to a monospace font. The "myclass" style is applied to the top heading and the bottom paragraph:

classstyle.html

```
<head>
<title>Class Styling</title>
<style type="text/css">
.myclass { font-family:monospace; color:red }
</style>
</head>
```

The class name must be preceded by a full stop when it is being defined in the stylesheet.

```
<body>
<h3 class="myclass">Archaeological Museum</h3>
<p>The most important collection of Minoan art and
artifacts in the world.</p>
<h3>Historical Museum</h3>
<p class="myclass">The history of Crete from Byzantine
to modern times.</p>
</body>
```

Styling with Identity

All HTML 4 tags that are used to display content can accept an attribute called **id** to which a name can be assigned.

The **id** name can be used to identify that individual tag in a stylesheet defining rules for how its content should appear.

In the example below all four paragraphs are assigned **id** names but only three of those are used in the stylesheet to assign rules to their contents:

idstyle.html

The id name must be preceded by a hash character (#) when defining rules in the stylesheet block.

```
<head>
<title>Id Styling</title>
<style type="text/css">
#para2 { font-family:cursive; color:red }
#para3 { font-family:serif; color:green }
#para4 { font-family:fantasy; color:blue }
</style>
</head>

<body>
<p id="para1">Paragraph 1 - Default</p>
<p id="para2">Paragraph 2 - Cursive</p>
<p id="para3">Paragraph 3 - Serif</p>
<p id="para4">Paragraph 4 - Fantasy</p>
</body>
```

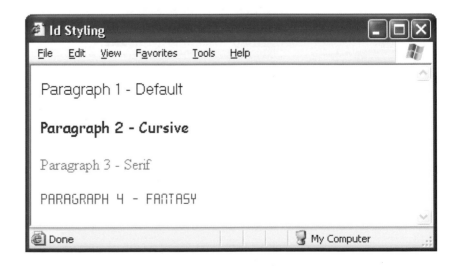

Colors

When assigning colors in HTML the color should be specified as a hexadecimal number preceded by a hash mark.

This six figure number represents the Red-Green-Blue (RGB) components that make up the whole color.

The first two numbers are its red component value, the second two numbers are its green component value and the third two numbers are its blue component value.

A hexadecimal color number that has zero RGB values creates Black with the hexadecimal number of #000000.

Conversely a hexadecimal number that has all maximum RGB values creates White with the hexadecimal #FFFFFF.

To create a red hexadecimal value you can use maximum R value plus zero GB values to produce hexadecimal #FF0000.

HTML 4 also recognizes the following 16 colors by name:

Name	Hexadecimal	Name	Hexadecimal
Black	#000000	Green	#008000
Silver	#C0C0C0	Lime	#00FF00
Gray	#808080	Olive	#808000
White	#FFFFFF	Yellow	#FFFF00
Maroon	#800000	Navy	#000080
Red	#FF0000	Blue	#0000FF
Purple	#800080	Teal	#008080
Fuchsia	#FF00FF	Aqua	#00FFFF

To assign any color a style sheet must be used with the hexadecimal number – or the color name if one of the above.

So "color:red;" and "color:#FF0000;" are both valid rules.

Applying color style

This example applies font and color style rules to two paragraphs in the document body.

The first rule in the style sheet changes the font for all paragraphs in the document.

Next the background and text colors are specified for the top paragraph using recognized name values.

Lastly the background and text colors are specified for the bottom paragraph using hexadecimal number values:

color.html

```
<head>
<title>Applying Color Style</title>
<style type="text/css">
p { font-family:cursive }
#para1 { color:yellow; background-color:blue }
#para2 { color:#FF0000; background-color:#FFFF00 }
</style>
</head>

<body>
<p id="para1">Paragraph 1 - Yellow on Blue</p>
<p id="para2">Paragraph 2 - Red on Yellow</p>
</body>
```

Internet Explorer sets the paragraph boundary across the page – other browsers may define the boundaries of the paragraph differently.

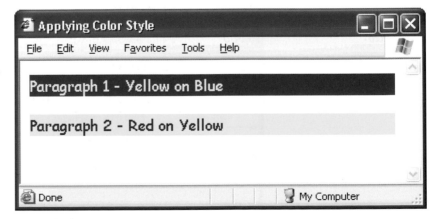

Dividing content

The document body can be divided into blocks by grouping its content elements with the **<div> </div>** tags.

This is very useful to control page layout as the style characteristics of each block can be set by stylesheet rules.

The **<div>** tag can have **id** and **class** attributes that may be used in the stylesheet to specify style requirements.

This example sets the background color of all **<div>** elements and the absolute position of two **<div>** blocks:

divstyle.html

```
<head> <title>Controlling Block Layout</title>
<style type="text/css">
div { background-color:yellow; color:red }
#div1 { position:absolute; top:0px; left:0px }
#div2 { position:absolute; top:30px; left:120px }
</style>
</head>
```

An absolutely positioned block will always maintain its set position regardless of other content.

```
<body>
<div id="div1"> <p>Paragraph 1</p> </div>
<div id="div2">
<p>Paragraph 2</p> <p>Paragraph 3</p>
</div>
</body>
```

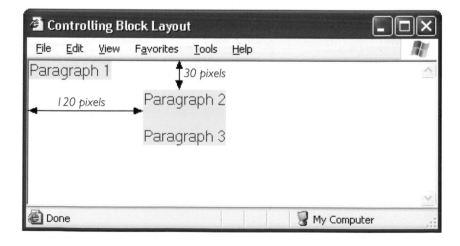

Centering with style

In HTML 4 the previous **<center>** tag, that was used to center content, has been made obsolete. Instead, the stylesheet **text-align** rule is now used to center document content.

An entire document can be made to align its content centrally by applying a stylesheet rule to its document body.

Individual blocks of content can be made to align their content by applying a style sheet rule to the **<div>** element.

In this example three blocks are centered on the page with each controlling alignment of their text individually:

align.html

```
<head>
<title>Style Alignment</title>
<style type="text/css">
body { text-align:center }
div { width:150; background-color:yellow; color:red }
#div1 { text-align:left }
#div2 { text-align:center }
#div3 { text-align:right }
</style>
</head>

<body>
<div id="div1"><p>Paragraph 1</p></div>
<div id="div2"><p>Paragraph 2</p></div>
<div id="div3"><p>Paragraph 3</p></div>
</body>
```

*Notice that there are automatic line breaks after each **<div>** block, but no line spaces between them.*

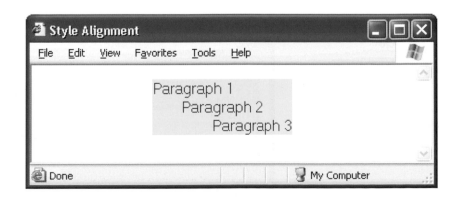

Inline styling

Style rules can be applied to small pieces of text "in-line" with **\<span> \</span>** tags.

These tags allow both **id** and **class** attributes to apply stylesheet rules without automatically adding line breaks.

Unlike the **\<div>** blocks that can be used to control block layout the **\<span>** tag is not used for positioning but rather to set display characteristics for short pieces of text.

This example uses **\<span>** tags to set the appearance of two pieces of text within a paragraph that is contained in a block:

spanstyle.html

```
<head>
<title>Span Styling</title>
<style type="text/css">
#div1 { width:300; background-color:teal; padding:5px;
                        color:white; font-weight:bold }
#span1 { background-color:yellow; color:red }
#span2 { background-color:blue; color:yellow }
</style>
</head>

<body>
<div id="div1"> <p>The road descends to
<span id="span1">Agios Nikolaos</span>
offering magnificent views of the
<span id="span2">Bay of Mirabello</span> </p> </div>
</body>
```

*The **\<span>** tag can also accept attributes for intrinsic events such as **onmouseover** and **onclick**, that can be used with scripts for dynamic effects.*

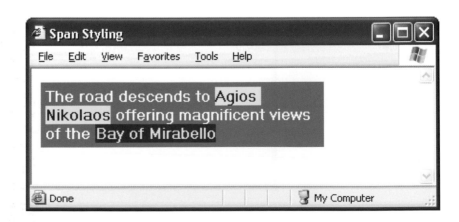

Lists and entities

This chapter illustrates by example how HTML can be used to display different types of lists in a variety of ways. There are also examples to demonstrate how entities can be used to add non-alphanumeric characters to the text.

Covers

Chapter Five

Unordered lists

A list of items that does not require the items to be numbered in order is known as an "unordered" list.

The unordered list tags **<ul> </ul>** are used to contain the items in an unordered list.

Each list item should be surrounded by **<li> </li>** tags, but the closing tag may optionally be omitted.

Browsers will choose how the list is to be presented but generally they will indent the list from other text. Unordered lists will start each item with a default bullet point selected by the browser.

The following example illustrates an unordered list that is indented with bullet points marking each list item:

list.html

*Use the **</li>** closing tag to make the code more readable.*

```
<head>
<title>Unordered List</title>
</head>

<body>
<p>First Unordered List:</p>
<ul>
<li>One</li>
<li>Two</li>
<li>Three</li>
</ul>
</body>
```

Bullet point styles

The style of bullet points to be used for marking items in an unordered list can be specified in the style sheet.

Bullet points may be either "square" or "circle", or a filled circle called a "disc".

This example illustrates each type of bullet point style:

bullets.html

```
<head>
<title>Bullet Point Styles</title>
<style type="text/css">
#list1 { list-style-type:disc; color:red }
#list2 { list-style-type:circle; color:green }
#list3 { list-style-type:square; color:blue }
</style>
</head>
```

*Notice that the stylesheet uses the **id** name of each list to apply the rule.*

```
<body>
<ul id="list1"><li>Disc 1</li><li>Disc 2</li></ul>
<ul id="list2"><li>Circle 1</li><li>Circle 2</li></ul>
<ul id="list3"><li>Square 1</li><li>Square 2</li></ul>
</body>
```

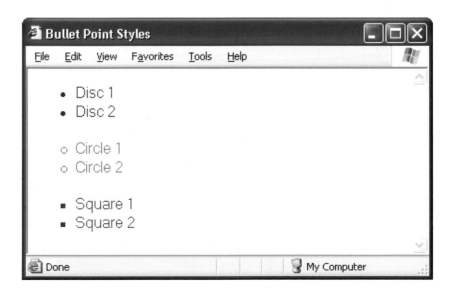

Ordered lists

A list of items that has each item numbered to note its position in the list is called an "ordered" list. The HTML **<ol>** and **</ol>** tags are used to contain the items in an ordered list. Each list item should be enclosed within **<li> </li>** tags and will be numbered in the default manner of the browser.

All lists can be nested, as seen in this example that demonstrates two nested ordered lists:

order.html

*The **</li>** tag may be omitted but its inclusion makes the code more readable.*

```
<head>
<title>Ordered Lists</title>
</head>

<body>
<ol>
<li>One</li>
<li>Two
    <ol>
    <li>Alpha</li>
    <li>Bravo</li>
    <li>Charlie</li>
    </ol>
</li>
<li>Three</li>
</ol>
</body>
```

Numbering styles

Ordered list number style can be specified as Arabic, lowercase or uppercase Roman, and lowercase or uppercase Alpha, as seen here:

numlist.html

```
<head>
<title>Numbering Styles</title>
<style type="text/css">
.arab { list-style-type:arabic-numbers; color:red }
.lwrR { list-style-type:lower-roman; color:green }
.uprR { list-style-type:upper-roman; color:blue }
.lwrA { list-style-type:lower-alpha; color:orange }
.uprA { list-style-type:upper-alpha; color:purple }
</style>
</head>

<body>
<ol class="lwrR">
<li>Lower Roman
    <ol>
    <li class="uprR">Upper Roman</li>
    <li class="arab">Arabic</li>
    <li class="lwrA">Lower Alpha</li>
    <li class="uprA">Upper Alpha</li>
    </ol>
</li>
<li>Lower Roman</li>
</ol>
</body>
```

Class attributes apply stylesheet rules to the entire first list and to each item in the nested list.

Definition lists

A definition list is a unique type of list where each list item consists of a term and a definition. All the list items are contained within **<dl> </dl>** tags.

The HTML **<dt>** and **</dt>** tags are used to contain a list term while **<dd> </dd>** tags contain a list definition. Closing tags are optional for both **<dt>** and **<dd>** tags.

Use closing tags **</dt>** *and* **</dd>** *to make the code more easily readable.*

The browser will choose how to display a definition list but generally Web browsers will add a line break after the **<dt>** term and offset the **<dd>** definition.

In this example a definition list is used to display simple definitions of some popular Web languages:

deflist.html

```
<head>
<title>Definition List</title>
</head>

<body>
<dl>
<dt>HTML4:</dt> <dd>Content markup language.</dd>
<dt>JavaScript:</dt>
<dd>Client-side scripting language.</dd>
<dt>Perl:<dt> <dd>Server-side scripting language.</dd>
</dl>
</body>
```

Use definition lists to display film scripts – where the **<dt>** *term is the speaker's name, and the* **<dd>** *definition is the dialog for that speaker.*

Horizontal rule

A horizontal ruled line can be drawn across the display area with the HTML **<hr>** tag.

This tag is used alone without any closing tag.

The line will be drawn across the available display space excluding any margins or padding borders that it meets.

In the example below the first **<hr>** line fills the window width excluding margins while the second**<hr>** line fills the **<div>** block, excluding padding borders:

hrule.html

```
<head>
<title>Horizontal Rule</title>
<style type="text/css">
#div1 { position:absolute; top:70; left:130;
        width:100; border:3px double red; padding:5px }
</style>
</head>

<body>
<p>Section 1</p>
<hr>
<p>Section 2</p>
<div id="div1">Section 3<hr>Section 4</div>
</body>
```

*The browser may choose how to display the **<hr>** line.*

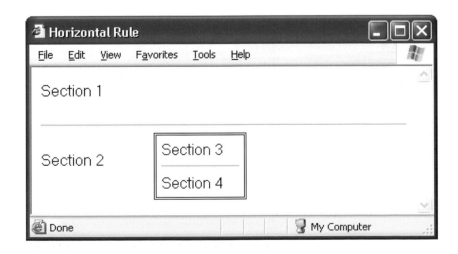

Character entities

The HTML specification provides entities as a means to display characters that are meaningful in HTML itself. This is necessary otherwise a "**<**" character within the general text would be seen as the start of a HTML tag by the browser.

Entity references always start with a "**&**" ampersand character and must be terminated by a semi-colon.

There are many character entities available in HTML including the Greek alphabet in both upper and lower case.

Those most frequently used are shown in this example:

entity.html

```
<head>
<title>Non Alpha-numeric Characters</title>
</head>

<body>
<p>
Space Here <br> Ampersand &amp; <br>
Less Than &lt;   <br> Greater Than &gt; <br>
Quote &quot;     <br> Copyright &copy; <br>
Registered &reg;<br> Trademark &trade;
</p>
</body>
```

For a full list of all character entities see the Entity References at www.w3c.org.

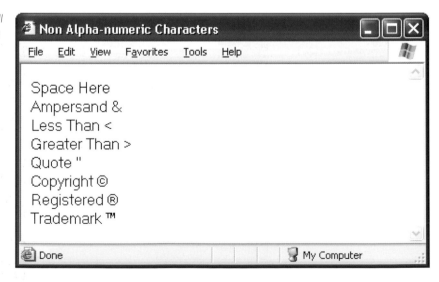

Making tables

This chapter describes the new table model introduced in HTML 4 that enables much faster display of table content. All the table tags are demonstrated to build a variety of tables that illustrate how to define rows, columns and cells.

Covers

Chapter Six

A simple table

Tables are used frequently to display information in HTML documents and are enclosed within **<table> </table>** tags.

Each piece of table data is contained in cells defined by the HTML **<td> </td>** tags and each row of cells is contained in **<tr> </tr>** tags.

The **<table>** tag accepts an attribute named **border** to assign a width of border to surround the table and each cell.

A caption can be displayed with the table using **<caption> </caption>** tags. If this tag is used it must immediately follow the opening **<table>** tag.

The example below creates a table together with a caption.

This table displays a **border** one pixel wide and has one row containing three table data cells:

table.html

```
<body>
<table border="1">
<caption>A Simple Table</caption>
<tr>
   <td>Cell 1</td>
   <td>Cell 2</td>
   <td>Cell 3</td>
</tr>
</table>
</body>
```

Later examples in this chapter build on this simple table as more table features are introduced.

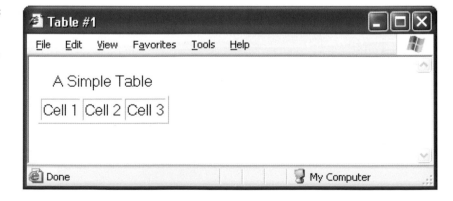

Formatting cells

Data in the table cells in the example opposite is positioned right up to the borders of each cell and the cells are spaced a short distance apart by default.

The appearance of the cell data can be improved by adding padding to each cell with a **\<table\> cellpadding** attribute. Also the spacing between cells may be specified with the **\<table\> cellspacing** attribute.

The background color can be specified in HTML 4 tables with a **style** attribute. This attribute can be used in the **\<table\>**, **\<tr\>** and **\<td\>** tags to set the background color respectively for the overall background, for a row of cells and the background color of individual cells.

This example builds on the previous table to add cell padding and spacing plus background color in two cells:

cells.html

```
<body>
<table border="1" cellpadding="5" cellspacing="5">
<caption>Formatting Cells</caption>
<tr>
  <td style="background-color:aqua">Cell 1</td>
  <td>Cell 2</td>
  <td style="background-color:fuchsia">Cell 3</td>
</tr>
</table>
</body>
```

Assign a table border width of zero to hide all the table and cell borders.

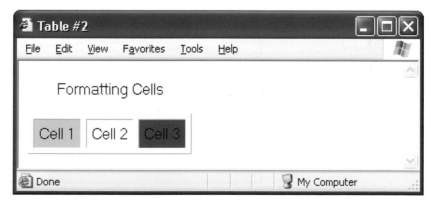

Positioning the table

To position a table on the page it can be contained within a **<div>** block to which an alignment style can be applied.

This allows a table to be positioned on the page just like any other block of document content.

The example below builds on the previous example to add a specific table width, using the **<table> width** attribute, and a **<div>** block to centre the table on the page:

position.html

```
<head> <title>Table #3</title>
<style type="text/css">
div { text-align:center }
</style>
</head>

<body>
<div>
<table border="1" width="250" cellpadding="5"
                              cellspacing="5">
<caption>Centered Table</caption>
<tr style="background-color:aqua">
  <td>Cell 1</td> <td>Cell 2</td> <td>Cell 3</td>
</tr>
</table>
</div>
</body>
```

The background color of the cells is set for the entire row in the <tr> tag.

Notice that although the table is central the text data in each cell is not.

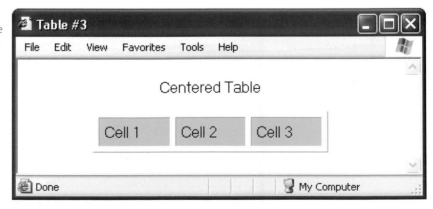

Adding rows

To add an additional row to a table requires another set of **<tr> </tr>** tags to be added containing the same number of **<td> </td>** cells as used in the first row.

This example builds on the previous example to add another row containing three cells and also adds another rule to the stylesheet to centre the data in all cells:

addrows.html

```
<head>
<title>Table #4</title>
<style type="text/css">
div { text-align:center }
td { text-align:center; background-color:aqua }
</style>
</head>
<body>
<div>
<table border="1" style="background-color:fuchsia"
        width="220" cellpadding="5" cellspacing="5" >
<caption>Adding Rows</caption>
<tr><td>Cell 1</td> <td>Cell 2</td> <td>Cell 3</td></tr>
<tr><td>Cell 4</td> <td>Cell 5</td><td>Cell 6 </td></tr>
</table>
</div>
</body>
```

*The background color is set for the entire table inside the **<table>** tag – but the cell background color is set in the stylesheet.*

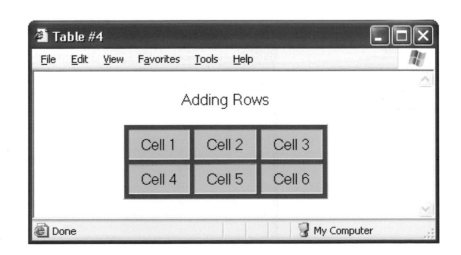

Spanning rows

A table cell can be made to span across a number of table rows with the **<td> rowspan** attribute. This attribute is assigned the number of rows to be spanned by the cell.

The cells being spanned in other rows must be removed.

In this example Cell 1 spans across two rows and Cell 4 has been removed:

rowspan.html

*This example builds on the previous example to show **rowspan**.*

```
<head>
<title>Table #5</title>
<style type="text/css">
div { text-align:center }
td  {  text-align:center; background-color:aqua }
</style>
</head>

<body>
<div> <table border="1" style="background-color:fuchsia"
          width="220" cellpadding="5" cellspacing="5">
<caption>Cell Spanning Rows</caption>
<tr>
<td rowspan="2" style="background-color:yellow">
Cell 1</td> <td>Cell 2</td> <td>Cell 3</td>
</tr>  <tr> <td>Cell 5</td><td>Cell 6</td> </tr>
</table> </div>
</body>
```

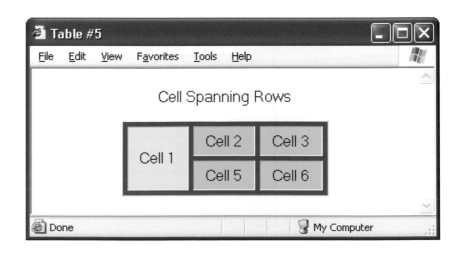

Spanning columns

A table cell can be made to span across a number of table columns with the **<td> colspan** attribute. This attribute is assigned the number of columns to be spanned by the cell.

The cells being spanned in other columns must be removed.

In this example Cell 2 spans across two columns and Cell 3 has been removed:

colspan.html

*This example builds on the previous example to show **colspan**.*

```
<head>
<title>Table #6</title>
<style type="text/css">
div { text-align:center }
td  {  text-align:center; background-color:aqua }
</style>
</head>

<body>
<div> <table border="1" style="background-color:fuchsia"
          width="220" cellpadding="5" cellspacing="5">
<caption>Cell Spanning Columns</caption>
<tr> <td rowspan="2" style="background-color:yellow">
Cell 1</td>
<td colspan="2" style="background-color:lime">
Cell 2</td> </tr>
<tr> <td>Cell 5</td><td>Cell 6</td></tr> </table> </div>
</body>
```

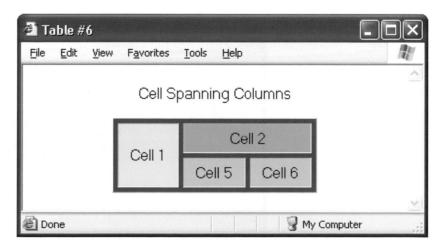

Header and footer

Extra rows can be added to the top and bottom of a table to display header and footer information.

The header row must be contained in **<thead> </thead>** tags and the footer row in tags named **<tfoot> </tfoot>**.

Cells in the header row may also use **<th> </th>** tags to contain their cell data instead of the usual **<td> </td>** tags. This will denote their data as header information.

When adding header and footer rows the rest of the regular rows must be contained within **<tbody> </tbody>** tags.

The simple table shown below includes a footer row and a header row containing column numbers:

headnfoot.html

```
<body>
<table border="1" cellspacing="1" width="350">
<thead style="background-color:yellow">
  <tr><th>Col 1</th><th>Col 2</th><th>Col 3</th></tr>
</thead>
<tfoot style="background-color:fuchsia">
  <tr><td colspan="3">Footer</td></tr>
</tfoot>
<tbody style="background-color:lime">
  <tr><td>Cell 1</td><td>Cell 2</td><td>Cell 3</td></tr>
</tbody> </table>
</body>
```

The browser may choose to display header information in a different way to regular cell data – here it's bold and centered.

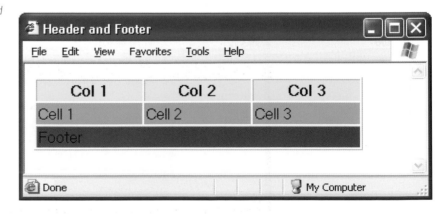

Cell content alignment

The position of data within a table cell can be controlled with two attributes of the **<td>** tag.

Horizontal alignment can be specified with the **align** attribute that may have a value of **"left"**, **"center"** or **"right"**.

If the horizontal alignment is not specified the data will normally be positioned horizontally at the left by default.

Vertical alignment can be specified with the **valign** attribute that may have a value of **"top"**, **"middle"** or **"bottom"**.

If the vertical alignment is not specified the data will normally be positioned vertically in the middle by default.

The example below creates a table illustrating how data alignment can be changed using the **align** and **valign** attributes:

aligndata.html

Specialized attributes and values for data alignment are given in the full specifications. For details see ***www.w3c.org***.

```
<body>
<table border="1" cellpadding="3"
                  cellspacing="0" width="350">
<tr>
<td align="center" valign="middle" style="color:red">
Center<br>Middle</td>
<td align="left" valign="top" style="color:green">
Top Left</td>
<td align="right" valign="bottom" style="color:blue">
Bottom Right</td>
</tr>
</table>
</body>
```

Cell style

Stylesheet rules can be applied to table cells and rows using either an **id** name, or a **class**, or both **id** name and **class**.

The example below applies rules to Cell1 with its **id** name and to Cell2 using a **class** name. Cell3 has style rules applied with both **id** and **class**

In the bottom row the font for all cells is specified in the stylesheet using the **id** name of the **\<tr\>** tag.

cellstyle.html

```
<head>
<title>Cell Style</title>
<style type="text/css">
#cell1 { background-color:yellow }
.lime { background-color:lime }
#cell3 { font-style:italic; background-color:fuchsia }
#row2 { font-family:monospace }
</style>
</head>
```

Use a stylesheet rule to set the overall background color of the table and its borders.

```
<body>
<table border="1" cellpadding="10" cellspacing="2">
<tr> <td id="cell1">Cell1</td>
    <td class="lime">Cell2</td>
    <td id="cell3" >Cell3</td> </tr>
<tr id="row2">
  <td>Cell4</td><td>Cell5</td><td>Cell6</td> </tr>
</table>
</body>
```

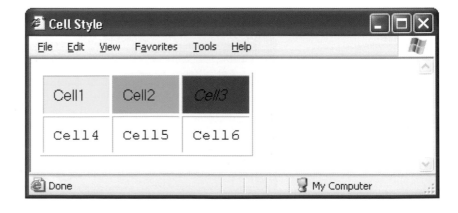

Table frame and rules

The appearance of a HTML 4 table can be customized using the **frame** and **rules** attributes of the **<table>** tag.

Possible values for these attributes are listed in the table below and the example demonstrates them in action:

By default browsers will normally display all these unless the table border width is set at zero.

Frame	Specifies	Rule	Specifies
above	top side only	groups	display ruled lines between table header, body and footer only
below	bottom side only		
hside	top and bottom only		
vsides	left and right only	cols	lines between rows
lhs	left-hand side only	rows	lines between columns
rhs	right-hand side only	all	lines between all rows and columns
box	all four sides		

framerule.html

```
<body>
<table border="1" cellpadding="3" cellspacing="2"
        width="250" frame="below" rules="cols">
<tr><td>Cell1</td><td>Cell2</td><td>Cell3</td></tr>
<tr><td>Cell4</td><td>Cell5</td><td>Cell6</td></tr>
</table>
</body>
```

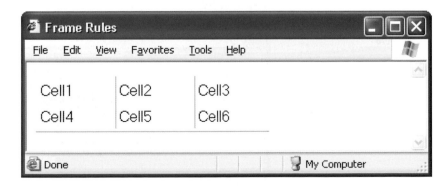

Grouping columns

Table columns may be grouped together so that style rules can be applied to all columns within the group.

The columns are grouped using **<colgroup> </colgroup>** tags together with their **span** attribute to assign the number of columns to be placed in that group.

In the example below the table has two column groups to which style rules have been applied:

group.html

```
<head>
<title>Column Groups</title>
<style type="text/css">
#group1 { background-color:yellow }
#group2 { color:white; background-color:purple }
</style>
</head>

<body>
<table border="1" cellpadding="3" cellspacing="2"
width="250">
<colgroup id="group1" span="2"></colgroup>
<colgroup id="group2"></colgroup>
<tr><td>Cell1</td><td>Cell2</td><td>Cell3</td></tr>
<tr><td>Cell4</td><td>Cell5</td><td>Cell6</td></tr>
<tr><td>Cell7</td><td>Cell8</td><td>Cell9</td></tr>
</table>
</body>
```

*If the span attribute is omitted the **<colgroup>** is assumed to span one column by default.*

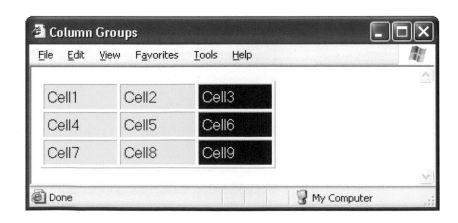

Column widths

To help the browser lay out a table more quickly all table column widths should be specified at the start of the table.

Column widths are defined, in pixels or as a percentage of overall table width, by the **width** attribute of a **<col>** tag.

The **<col>** tag does not have a closing tag.

A **span** attribute in the **<col>** tag may assign a number of columns to which its **width** value should apply.

This table uses 100% of total available width (excluding margins) with columns of 25%, 25% and 50% of the total:

width.html

```
<head>
<title>Column Widths</title>
<style type="text/css">
#col1 { color:white; background-color:purple }
#col2 { background-color:lime }
</style>
</head>
```

All the <col> tags for a table can optionally be contained inside a pair of <colgroup> </colgroup> tags.

```
<body>
<table border="1" cellpadding="3"
              cellspacing="2" width="100%">
<col id="col1" span="2" width="25%">
<col id="col2" width="50%">
<tr><td>Cell1</td><td>Cell2</td><td>Cell3</td></tr>
<tr><td>Cell4</td><td>Cell5</td><td>Cell6</td></tr>
</table>
</body>
```

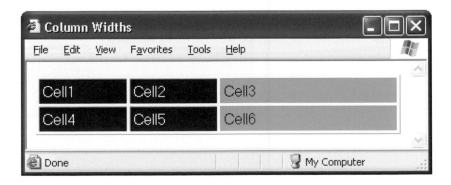

Summary attribute

For the benefit of non-visual browsers all **<table>** tags should include a descriptive **summary** attribute, like the one seen here:

summary.html

```
<head>  <title>Sample Table</title>
<style type="text/css">
table { text-align:center }
th    { background-color:purple; color:white }
td    { background-color:lime }
</style>
</head>

<body>
<table border="0" cellpadding="3" cellspacing="2"
       width="250" summary="Tyre Pressure Conversions">
<caption>Tyre Pressures</caption>
<colgroup><col width="125"><col width="125"></colgroup>
<thead>  <tr><th>lb/sq.in</th>
      <th>kg/cm<sup><small>2</small></sup></th></tr>  </thead>
<tbody>
   <tr><td>26</td><td>1.8</td></tr>
   <tr><td>28</td><td>2.0</td></tr>
   <tr><td>30</td><td>2.2</td></tr>
</tbody>
</table>
</body>
```

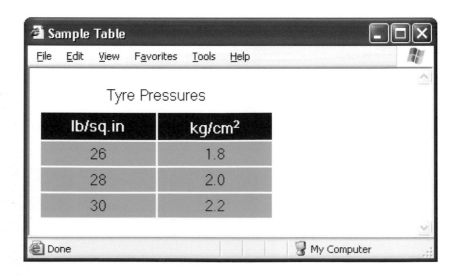

Hyperlinks and anchors

This chapter explains the special ability of HTML to define hyperlinks that enable users to navigate around the Web. There are examples showing how HTML tags can specify content as an anchor or a hyperlink to a variety of targets.

Covers

Chapter Seven

Creating hyperlinks

Text or an image in a document body can become a hyperlink "anchor" when contained in **<a> </a>** tags that specify a destination for that link.

The destination is assigned to an attribute of the **<a>** tag called **href** and may be an absolute or relative address.

In the browser the hyperlink is displayed in a manner that distinguishes the link from regular document content.

The destination may be any type of file that the browser can recognize.

For example, text that is a hyperlink may be displayed as reverse video, different color or underlined. Images that are hyperlinks are often displayed with a colored border.

In a Web browser the link destination address will generally be displayed in the windows status bar whenever the user places the pointer over a hyperlink anchor.

The example below illustrates a text hyperlink that will open a destination document when the user follows the link:

page1.html

```
<head>
<title>Page 1</title>
</head>

<body>
<p>Click<a href="http://localhost/page2.html">here</a>
to open Page 2.
</p>
</body>
```

*The **localhost** domain in this example is the default domain name for a web server on the local system. Omit the **http://localhost/** prefix to link as **href = "page2.html"** if the page2.html file is within the same directory as the page1.html file.*

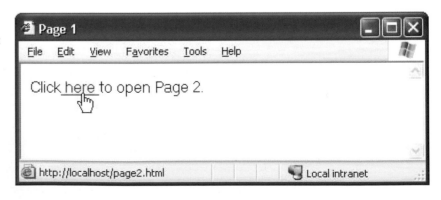

Following links

HTML 4 provides three means to follow hyperlinks:

Pointer

Use a mouse, trackball or similar device to place a screen pointer over the link then click to load the new document.

Tab

Use a Tab key to navigate across the links in a document then hit Enter to load the new document. Typically the tab order follows the order in which links appear on the page.

Access Key

The accesskey attribute may also be used in <area>, <label>, <textarea>, <input>, <legend> and <button> elements.

Use a designated character key to load the new document. The key is specified with the **accesskey** attribute of the **<a>** element and pressing the key gives focus to the link.

The method of entering the access key will vary according to platform. For instance Windows users must press Alt+access key, and Mac users must press Cmd+access key.

In the example below an access key has been added to the code on the facing page. Entering the access key (Alt+x) gives focus to the link, then pushing the Enter key loads the page.

accesskey.html

```
<head>
<title>Page 1</title>
</head>

<body>
<p><a href="http://localhost/page2.html" accesskey="x">
    Hit access key x</a> to open page 2.
</p>
</body>
```

Fragment anchors

A hyperlink destination can be specified as another point in the current document using fragment anchors.

The fragment anchor is created with the **name** attribute of the **<a>** tag which is assigned a given name.

Hyperlinks may then use this name preceded by a hash character (#) as a link destination.

A document may contain innumerable fragment anchors but each name must be unique.

When the user follows a link to a fragment anchor the browser window generally displays the document starting from the point where the anchor is located.

This type of hyperlink is often seen at the end of long documents to provide a return to the top of the page.

In the example below the start of the document creates a fragment anchor and the end of the document provides a hyperlink to jump back to it:

fragment.html

```
<body>
<p> <a name="top_of_page">Welcome</a> </p>

<!-- long document content -->

<p> <a href="#top_of_page">Top of Page</a> </p>
</body>
```

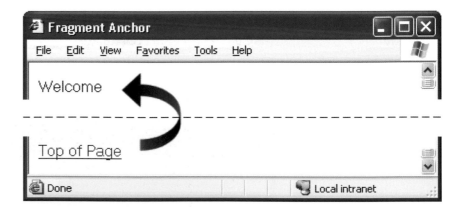

Link to element

In HTML 4 the **id** attribute of any content tag can be used to specify the destination of a hyperlink.

The tag's **id** attribute is assigned a given name that can be used with a leading hash character to specify a link destination.

The entire document is loaded but the window is automatically scrolled down to the location of the fragment identifier.

This name is more correctly called a "fragment identifier" and can be used to navigate around a document in the same way as the example on the opposite page.

A hyperlink can load another document to display in the window at the point where a fragment identifier is located.

In this example a hyperlink in one document opens a second document at the location of a fragment identifier:

```
<head> <title>Page A</title> </head>
<body>
<p><a href="pageB.html#line2">Page B - Line 2</a></p>
</body>
```

pageA.html

```
<head> <title>Page B</title> </head>
<body>
<p id="line1">This is line 1</p>
<p id="line2">This is line 2</p>
<p id="line3">This is line 3</p>
</body>
```

pageB.html

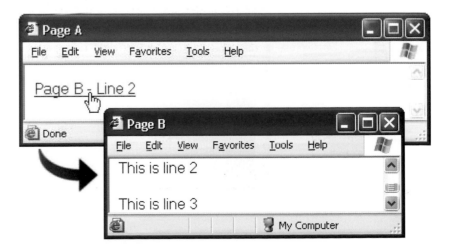

Link title tooltip

The **title** attribute of an **<a>** anchor tag can be useful to provide information about the destination of a hyperlink.

When the user moves the pointer over a hyperlink the browser may display the **title** attribute value as a tooltip.

title.html

```
<body>
<p>Add more excitement to your pages -<br>
Learn client-side scripting with<br>
<a href="jsies.gif"
        title="Click here to view the book cover">
JavaScript in easy steps</a> </p>
</body>
```

The destination can be any type of recognized file – a GIF file is used here.

Link to protocol

Hyperlinks may target a script function rather than a URL location address.

The link must specify the protocol name followed by a colon then the function name that is to be called.

Most typically this will be a call to a JavaScript function using the protocol specifier **javascript:**.

This feature is extremely useful in the creation of interactive Web pages to respond to user actions.

In the following example the hyperlink destination uses a protocol specifier to call a JavaScript function that will display the current date and time in an alert dialog box:

protocol.html

```
<body>
<p>
<!-- PopUp Date & Time -->
<a href="javascript:alert(new Date().toGMTString())">
Click to show current date and time</a>
</p>
</body>
```

Hyperlinks can also use other recognized protocols for the destination.

Images as hyperlinks

Images can be used to create a hyperlink in place of regular text by surrounding the image tag with **<a>** anchor tags.

Most browsers will automatically indicate that the image is a hyperlink by adding a border around the image.

This may look unattractive on a Web page but the image borders can be removed if the stylesheet sets their **border-width** to zero.

The following example displays a text hyperlink and two image hyperlinks where one image is made border-less:

imagelink.html

```
<head>
<title>Image Links</title>
<style type="text/css">
.noborder { border-width:0 }
</style>
</head>

<body>
<p> <a href="page2.html">Click Here</a>
<a href="page2.html">
<img src="click.gif" width="60" height="60" alt="Click">
</a>
<a href="page2.html">
<img src="click.gif" width="60" height="60" alt="Click"
class="noborder"></a> </p>
</body>
```

For more on images in HTML documents – see page 88.

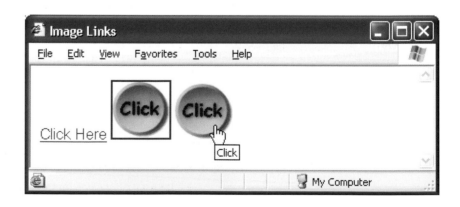

Image map hyperlinks

A single image can have multiple hyperlink destinations if an image map is added to define distinct areas for each link.

To add an image map the image tag must assign the map name preceded by a hash character to its **usemap** attribute.

Notice that the active border surrounds the whole image – not each link.

The map is contained within **<map> </map>** tags which have a **name** attribute to specify a given name for the map.

Each distinct area of the image that is to become a hyperlink is defined within the maps **<area>** tags that state the coordinates of the area, its shape and link destination.

This example uses one image map to create three hyperlinks:

imagemap.html

```
<body> <p>
<img src="trio.gif" usemap="#trio" alt="Trio Image">
<map name="trio">
<area shape="circle" coords="62,21,18" href="p1.html"
    alt="Link to page 1">
<area shape="circle" coords="28,79,18" href="p2.html"
    alt="Link to page 2">
<area shape="circle" coords="97,79,18" href="p3.html"
    alt="Link to page 3">
</map>
</p> </body>
```

Hyperlinks can be used to call script functions – see page 83.

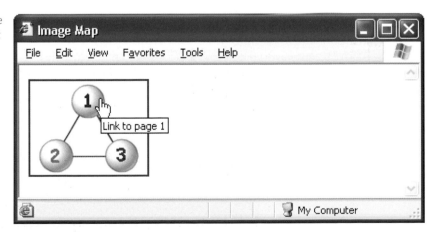

Mapping coordinates

The **shape** attribute of an **<area>** tag can define an image area as either **"circle"**, **"rect"** (rectangle) or **"poly"** (polygon).

Coordinate values assigned to the **coords** attribute in the **<area>** tag will vary according to the shape specified.

The table below lists the coordinates required by each shape:

The image map example on the previous page uses the circle shape to create the hyperlink "hotspots".

Shape	Coordinates
rect	left-x, top-y, right-x, bottom-y
circle	center-x, center-y, radius
poly	x1, y1, x2, y2, x3, y3,etc - one pair for each point. The first point and the final point must have identical coordinates to join up the shape

Calculating coordinates manually can be a difficult task. Fortunately modern graphics programs like Adobe Photoshop and Paint Shop Pro are able to generate image map code that can simply be pasted into the appropriate HTML document.

There are also inexpensive image mapping applications available such as the CoffeeCup image mapper shown here:

Find out more about the CoffeeCup image mapper on the Web at www.coffeecup.com.

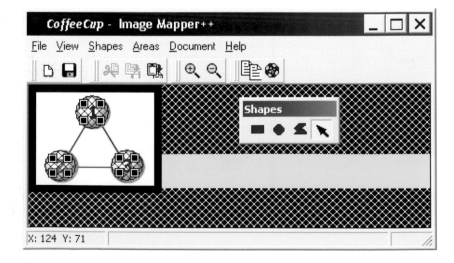

Embedding contents

This chapter demonstrates how to create a content-rich page by adding diverse content into a HTML document. There are examples that incorporate other text and HTML documents plus images, Java applets, animation and video.

Covers

Chapter Eight

Add an image

The HTML **<img>** tag can be used to add images to the content of a document body.

An **<img>** image element does not have a closing tag.

There are however a number of attributes that must be supplied inside an **<img>** tag for it to be valid.

*The image file location may be assigned to the **src** attribute as either a relative or absolute address.*

A **src** attribute should be assigned the address of the image to be displayed and an **alt** attribute must specify a text alternative in case the browser cannot display the image.

The dimensions to display the image must be assigned to the respective **width** and **height** attributes. These do not need to be the actual image dimensions as the browser will resize an image to suit the specified size.

In order for a script to reference an image it is important to assign a name to the image with the **<img>** id attribute.

The following example demonstrates an image tag called **"pic1"** with correctly specified attributes:

image.html

```
<head>
<title>Image Tags</title>
</head>

<body>
<p> <img id="pic1" src="fun.gif" width="200"
        height="60" alt="HTML is Fun"> </p>
</body>
```

Images with maps

A map can be specified with the **usemap** attribute of the **<img>** tag to react to the user of a HTML document.

The example below assigns lines of script to **onmouseout** and **onmouseover** attributes that display simple messages:

mapimage.html

```
<head>
 <title>Image With Map</title>
</head>

<body>
<p>
<img id="pic1" src="areas.gif" width="200"
          height="50" alt="Areas" usemap="#nums">

<map name="nums">
<area shape="rect" coords="0,0,100,50" href="a1.html"
onmouseout="document.forms.f.txt.value=''" alt="Area 1"
onmouseover="document.forms.f.txt.value='Area 1'">
<area shape="rect" coords="100,0,200,50" href="a2.html"
onmouseout="document.forms.f.txt.value=''"alt="Area 2"
onmouseover="document.forms.f.txt.value='Area 2'">
</map>
</p>
<form name="f" action="" method="post">
<p> <input name="txt" type="text" value=""> </p>
</form>
</body>
```

If the image uses a map all the **<area>** *tags must also have* **alt** *attributes to specify alternative text.*

Form elements are covered in detail later – see chapter 10.

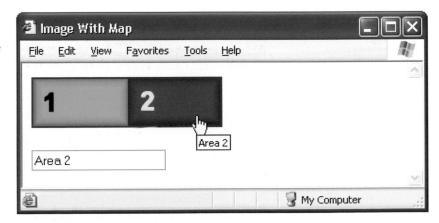

Objects and mime types

HTML 4 introduces the **<object> </object>** tags as a means to embed resources into a HTML document.

The **<object>** tag may use its **width** and **height** attributes to specify the display dimensions of the resource.

Most importantly its **data** attribute will specify the object location and its **type** attribute will describe a MIME type.

A Multipurpose Internet Mail Extension (MIME) is a registered description of a resource that can be universally recognized by all Web browsers.

The table below lists some of the MIME types that are most frequently used to describe common resources:

For details of all the many MIME types – see the W3C Web site online at

www.w3c.org.

MIME Type	Object Type
image/gif	GIF image resource
image/jpeg	JPG, JPEG, JPE image resource
image/png	PNG image resource
text/plain	TXT regular text document
text/html	HTM, HTML markup text documents
text/css	CSS cascading style sheet
text/javascript	JS javascript script resource
audio/x-wav	WAV sound resource
audio/x-mpeg	MP3 music resource
video/mpeg	MPEG, MPG, MPE video resource
video/x-msvideo	AVI video resource
application/java	CLASS java resource
application/pdf	PDF portable document

Embed an image object

The **<object> </object>** tags enable all kinds of content to become embedded into a HTML 4 document.

The location of the data to be embedded is assigned to an **<object>** attribute called **data** and the **type** attribute is assigned its MIME type.

An alternative text description can be contained between the tags to be displayed if the object cannot be embedded.

This example attempts to embed a GIF image into a HTML 4 document and the browser screenshots illustrate the result of both failure and success:

embed.html

```
<head>
<title>Embedded Image Object</title>
</head>

<body>
<p><object data="lilguy.gif" type="image/gif" width="29"
height="24">[Lilguy Image]<br> </object>
This is an embedded image object. </p>
</body>
```

Internet Explorer may insist on adding scroll bars – which can cause problems with the display of small embedded images.

*All alternative content between the **<object>** tags is ignored unless the object is not embedded.*

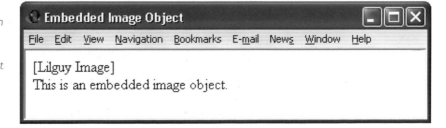

Embed a text file object

A plain text file can be embedded into a HTML 4 document with **<object>** tags in the same way as embedded images.

Here the MIME type is specified as **"text/plain"** and the alternative text provides a hyperlink to the text file:

text.html

```
<head>
<title>Embedded Text File Object</title>
</head>

<body>
<p>This is text in the main document that<br>
<object id="obj1" data="text.txt"
    type="text/plain" width="250" height="70">
[Click <a href="text.txt">here</a> for details]
</object> <br>continues around embedded objects. </p>
</body>
```

Notice that the displayed text retains a line break from the original file.

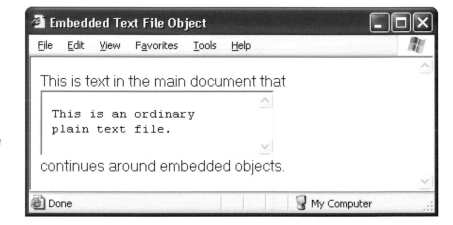

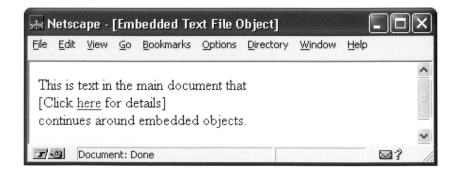

Embed a HTML object

HTML 4 documents can embed other HTML files by using **<object>** tags together with the MIME type of **"text/html"**. This example usefully demonstrates how to embed another HTML document from a remote location:

html.html

```
<head>
<title>Embedded HTML Object</title>
</head>

<body>
<p>This is text in the main document that <br>
<object data="content.html" type="text/html"
     width="300" height="80">
[Click <a href="http://fardomain/content.html">here </a>
for more details] </object>
<br>continues around the inline frame.</p>
</body>
```

Note that the embedded object area automatically has a scroll bar.

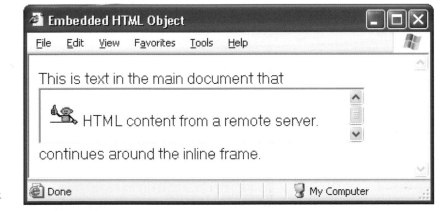

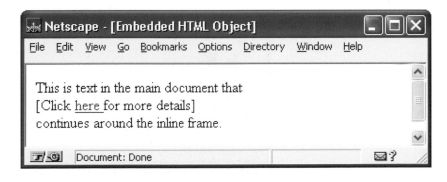

Embed a Java applet

An **\<object\>** tag attribute called **classid** can be used to embed a Java applet into a HTML 4 document.

The **classid** attribute is assigned the **"java:"** protocol specifier incorporating the name of the Java class.

As usual the **data** attribute specifies the file location.

When **classid** is used the regular **type** attribute should be replaced by a **codetype** attribute to specify the MIME type.

In the example below the Java class file called "hello.class" is assigned to the **classid** attribute, but without its file extension.

Also the **codetype** attribute identifies the MIME type to the browser as a Java applet:

java.html

```
<body>
<p>This is text in the main document that
<br>
<object id="applet1" classid="java:hello"
        data="hello.class"
        codetype="application/java"
        height="73" width="320">
[Java Applet]</object>
<br>continues around embedded objects.
</p>
</body>
```

The default text between the \<object\> tags is only to be displayed when the applet cannot be run.

Add applet parameters

Java applets that have variable parameters may have their initial values set with the HTML **<param>** tag. This tag has no closing tag but all **<param>** tags are contained in the applet's **<object>** tags. Parameter names that are recognized by the Java code can be assigned to the **<param> name** attribute. Then its **value** attribute can specify an initial value for use by the Java code.

This example sets many initial applet parameters:

param.html

```
<body>
<p>This is text in the main document that<br>
<object classid="java:billsClock"
  codetype="application/java" width="100" height="100">
<param name="bgcolor"       value="FFFFFF">
<param name="facecolor"     value="FFFF00">
<param name="sweepcolor"    value="FF0000">
<param name="minutecolor"   value="008080">
<param name="hourcolor"     value="000080">
<param name="textcolor"     value="000000">
<param name="casecolor"     value="800080">
<param name="trimcolor"     value="C0C0C0">
<param name="logoimageurl" value="java.gif">
[Java Applet]</object>
<br>continues around embedded objects.</p>
</body>
```

This applet ullows you to specify color components of a clock face and an image file for the logo.

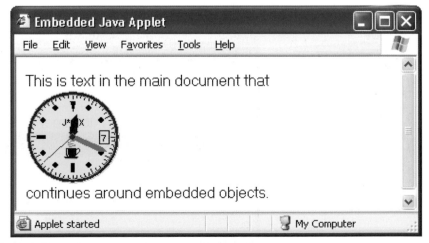

Embedding multimedia

Sound and video files can be assigned to the **href** attribute in a hyperlink so that when that link is followed the browser will call upon a local "helper" application associated with that file type. For instance, following the hyperlink below, on a Windows system, typically opens Windows Media Player to play the audio file:

```
<a href="music.mp3">Play me</a>
```

Set "autoStart" to "true" and "playCount" to "2" to play a sound file twice when the document loads. Set the "width" and "height" attributes to zero to hide the control panel.

The HTML 4 **<object> </object>** tags allow for all types of multimedia resources to be actually embedded in a document. Browsers then determine if they can handle an embedded multimedia resource or if they must call upon a helper application. Windows users can neatly use Microsoft's ActiveX controls to incorporate a media player console within a web page.

This example includes an ActiveX control that embeds a console to play a sound file within the HTML document:

audio.html

```
<body>
<p>This is text in the main document that<br>
<object id="Player1" width="250" height="65"
 classid="clsid:6BF52A52-394A-11d3-B153-00C04F79FAA6">
<param name="URL" value="sound.wav">
<param name="autoStart" value="false">
<param name="playCount" value="1">
[Click <a href="sound.wav">here</a> for sound]</object>
<br>continues around embedded objects.</p>
</body>
```

The default text and hyperlink, in square brackets, will be displayed in the event that the media player cannot be displayed.

The **<object>** tag has a number of attributes that assign a unique **id** to the object and specify its **width** and **height** on the page. The type of ActiveX control is determined by the value assigned to its **classid** attribute. Options are set with the **<param>** tag attributes that specify the source file name and how the player should work.

Similarly, this example embeds an ActiveX video player console within a web page to allow the user to play a MPEG video file:

video.html

```
<body>
<p>This is text in the main document that<br>
<object id="Player1" height="216" width="240"
 classid="clsid:6BF52A52-394A-11d3-B153-00C04F79FAA6">
<param name="uiMode" value="full">
<param name="URL" value="movie.mpg">
<param name="autoStart" value="false">
[Click <a href="movie.mpg">here</a> for movie]</object>
<br>continues around embedded objects.</p>
</body>
```

Notice the "uiMode" parameter that alters controls – other values are "none", "mini" or "invisible".

Microsoft Internet Explorer supports the <object> element defined in HTML4 – but other browsers are less compliant. Always provide a hyperlink to allow users of other browsers to play the media file.

QuickTime media player

The ActiveX control used in the previous example is bundled with the Windows operating system, so is available by default. Other ActiveX controls can be provided by installing browser plug-ins. For instance, a plug-in is available from Apple to support their QuickTime media format. Once installed, an ActiveX control is available that can be used to create a QuickTime media player embedded within a HTML document.

The example below embeds the QuickTime player and is similar to the previous example that embedded Windows media player. It simply adds a **codebase** attribute, stating the location of the plug-in, and specifies its parameters using different keyword values.

qtime.html

```
<body>
<p>This is text in the main document that<br>
<object width="240" height="180"
 classid="clsid:02BF25D5-8C17-4B23-BC80-D3488ABDDC6B"
 codebase="http://www.apple.com/qtactivex/qtplugin.cab">
<param name="src" value="rocket.mov">
<param name="autoplay" value="true">
<param name="controller" value="true">
[Click <a href="rocket.mov">here</a> for movie]</object>
<br>continues around embedded objects.</p>
</body>
```

QuickTime is the media format favored by Apple Mac users. You can discover more about QuickTime on the Apple website at www.apple.com/quicktime.

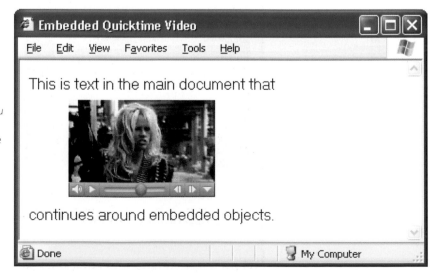

Real media player

Similarly this page embeds a Real media player Active X control:

real.html

The Real player requires separate objects for the "imagewindow" and the "controlpanel". The values assigned to the "console" parameters must be the same in each case to link the two parts together.

```
<body>
<p>This is text in the main document that<br>
<object id="screen" width="240" height="180"
classid="clsid:cfcdaa03-8be4-11cf-b84b-0020afbbccfa">
<param name="src" value="sample.rm">
<param name="controls" value="imagewindow">
<param name="autostart" value="false">
<param name="console" value="one">
[Click <a href="sample.rm">here</a> for movie]</object>
<br>
<object id="console" width="240" height="36"
 classid="clsid:cfcdaa03-8be4-11cf-b84b-0020afbbccfa">
<param name="controls" value="controlpanel">
<param name="console" value="one">
</object>
<br>continues around embedded objects.</p>
</body>
```

*Real is a high-quality player that enjoys cross-platform support. You can discover more about the Real One media player on the Real website at **www.real.com**.*

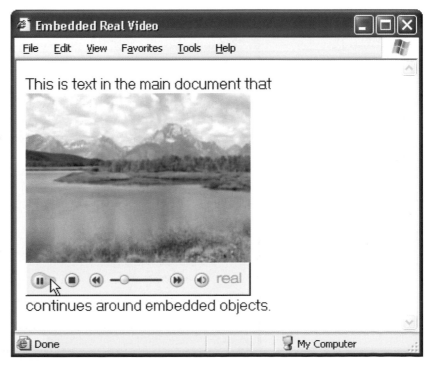

Flash movie player

The **<object>** tag is also used to embed Macromedia Flash movies in HTML 4 documents. Once the Flash plug-in is installed its ActiveX control can be assigned to the **<object> classid** attribute.

This example plays a Flash movie named **"picker.swf"** that has sliders which allow the user to mix different amounts of red, green and blue to make a color. When the button marked "Apply" is pressed the car image gets painted in the current mixed color.

flash.html

```
<body>
<p>This is text in the main document that<br>
<object id="color" width="360" height="270"
   classid="clsid:D27CDB6E-AE6D-11cf-96B8-444553540000">
<param name="movie" value="picker.swf">
</object>
<br>continues around embedded objects.</p>
</body>
```

Over 97% of web users have the Macromedia Flash player. You can discover more about Flash on the Macromedia website at ***www.macromedia.com***.

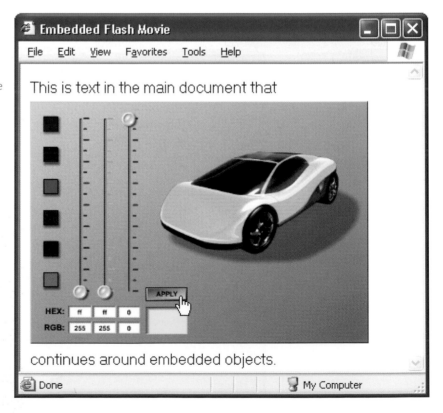

Using frames

This chapter demonstrates how to create multi-document pages with frames. There are examples that illustrate control of the frames' appearance to define how the whole page should appear in a Web browser.

Covers

Chapter Nine

The frameholder document

Frames provide a way to display multiple HTML documents in a single browser window.

This means that some documents can remain on display while others in a different frame are changed.

Typically a window might have three frames consisting of a top banner frame, a left-side menu frame and a main frame containing the changing page content.

The frames could occupy the window like this:

This frame arrangement is demonstrated on page 105.

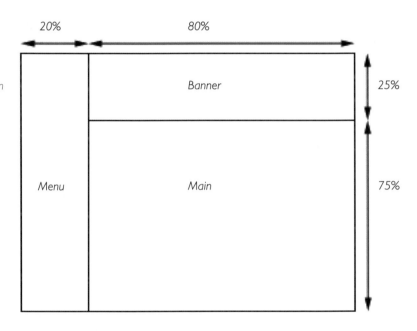

Each frameholder document in this chapter begins with a special frameset DTD like the one for HTML version 4.01 shown here. These are omitted in the listed code examples to save space but must begin actual code in order for it to be valid.

The arrangement of the frames is controlled by **<frameset>** and **</frameset>** tags in a dedicated frameholder HTML document.

Frameholder documents consist of a **<head>** section and a **<frameset>** section and must start with a special DTD like this:

```
<!DOCTYPE HTML PUBLIC
"-//W3C//DTD HTML 4.01 Frameset//EN"
"http://www.w3.org/TR/html4/frameset.dtd">
```

Two-column frameset

The **<frameset> </frameset>** tags control the horizontal allocation of frame width with a **cols** attribute.

Values assigned to the **cols** attribute may be expressed either as pixels or as a percentage where total width is 100%.

The frame values are assigned to the **cols** attribute from left to right as a comma-delimited list.

The **<frame>** *tag does not have any closing tag.*

Alternatively a wildcard value can be assigned with a **"★"**. This is most useful when the other frames are assigned set pixel values to mean "the available remaining width".

The **<frameset>** tags contain **<frame>** tags that specify the location of each frame document with their **src** attribute.

This example frameholder document arranges the window to display two frames as 20% and 80% of total available width:

twocols.html

```
<head>
<title>Two Column Frameset</title>
</head>

<frameset cols="20%,80%">

   <frame src="menu.html">

   <frame src="main.html">

</frameset>
```

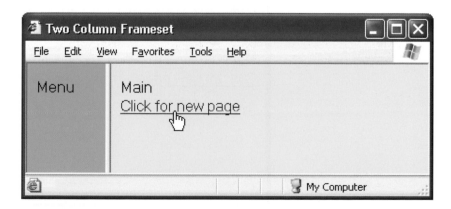

Two-row frameset

The **<frameset> </frameset>** tags control the vertical allocation of frame height with a **rows** attribute.

Values assigned to the **rows** attribute may be expressed either as pixels or as a percentage where total height is 100%.

The frame values are assigned to the **rows** attribute from left to right as a comma-delimited list.

Alternatively a wildcard value can be assigned with a "**★**". This is most useful when the other frames are assigned set pixel values to mean "the available remaining height".

This example frameholder document arranges the window to display two frames as 25% and 75% of total available height:

tworows.html

```
<head>
<title>Two Row Frameset</title>
</head>

<frameset rows="25%,75%">
   <frame src="banner.html">
   <frame src="main.html">
</frameset>
```

Note that this frameset arrangement could have used the wildcard as rows="25%," or (equally) rows="*,75%".*

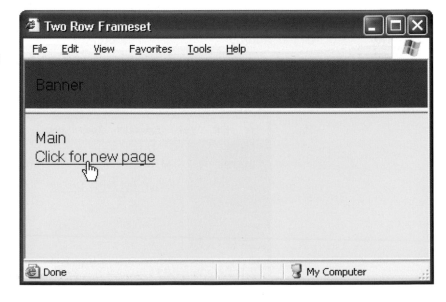

Nested frameset

Frameholder documents can contain nested framesets to provide a more elaborate arrangement of frames.

An initial **\<frameset\>** could, for instance, assign column widths to two frames. The second **\<frame\>** could be replaced with a nested **\<frameset\>** that might then assign row heights to two frames.

This arrangement is illustrated in the example below that creates a window containing a total of three frames:

threeframes.html

```
<head>
<title>Nested Frameset</title>
</head>

<frameset cols="20%,80%">

  <frame src="menu.html">

  <frameset rows="25%,75%">
    <frame src="banner.html">
    <frame src="main.html">
  </frameset>

</frameset>
```

This example combines the previous two examples and follows the frame layout on page 102.

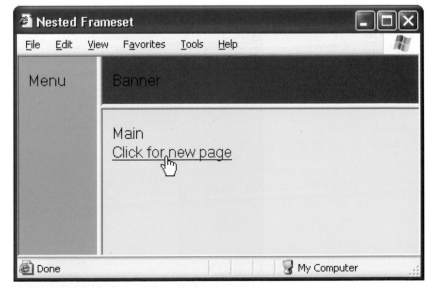

Frame appearance

If a border is not required between frames set the **\<frame\>** **frameborder** attribute to zero. If scroll bars are not required assign a value of **"no"** to its **scrolling** attribute.

Positioning of the frames contents from the frames edges can be specified by assigning positive pixel values to the **\<frame\>** attributes **marginwidth** and **marginheight**.

A frames dimension can be made permanent by adding the single-word attribute **noresize** into its **\<frame\>** tag.

This example removes all frame borders and the banner-frame scrollbars from the example on the previous page:

noborder.html

```
<head>
<title>Nested Frameset</title>
</head>

<frameset cols="20%,80%" border="0">
<frame src="menu.html" frameborder="0">
<frameset rows="25%,75%">
<frame src="banner.html" frameborder="0" scrolling="no">
<frame src="main.html" frameborder="0">
</frameset>
</frameset>
```

Although not compliant with the HTML 4 specifications, browser issues make it necessary to add **border="0"** *in the first* **\<frameset\>** *to hide borders.*

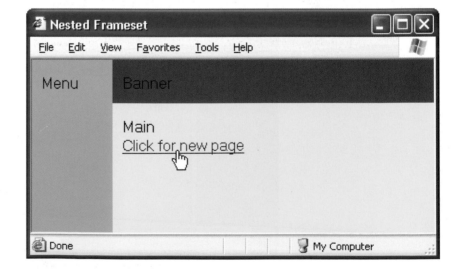

Frame targets

Hyperlinks, in any frame, treat the frame as a separate window and will load new location pages in that same frame.

Previously a **target** attribute could be used inside **<a>** elements to specify which frame should load a new page.

Future browser devices may not be able to display framed documents.

This attribute has not been included in the Strict HTML 4 specifications in order to discourage the use of frames.

Scripting may be used to specify which frame should load new location pages – so hyperlinks in a Menu frame could load new documents into a Main frame.

This example illustrates the normal method of loading:

main.html

```
<head>
<title>Main Frame</title>
</head>

<body>
<p>Main<br>
<a href="newpage.html">Click for new page</a>
</p>
</body>
```

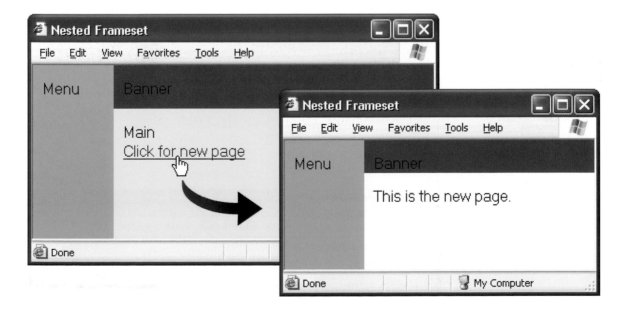

Alternative content

Using framed windows to display multiple documents is considered to be bad practice by many people. As the diversity of browsers increases it may be that framed windows are made obsolete.

In order to accommodate browsers that cannot display frames, or that have the frame facility disabled by user preferences, it is a good idea to provide an alternative.

The **<noframes>** and **</noframes>** tags can be used in a frameholder document to contain content that will be displayed when the frames cannot be loaded.

In the example below the **<noframes>** tags provide a notice explaining why the page did not load and offer a hyperlink to visit an alternative unframed page:

noframes.html

```
<head>
<title>Nested Frameset</title>
</head>

<frameset cols="20%,80%" border="0">
<frame name="menu" src="menu.html" frameborder="0">
<frameset rows="25%,75%">
<frame name="banner" src="banner.html"
                      frameborder="0" scrolling="no">
<frame name="main" src="main.html" frameborder="0">
  </frameset>

<noframes>This page uses frames.<br>
Click <a href="noframepage.html">here</a>
for a frameless version of the page
</noframes>
</frameset>
```

The W3C may have separated the frameset document with the intention of making frames obsolete at some point in the future.

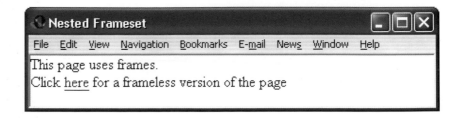

Creating forms

This chapter illustrates how HTML forms can submit data to a Web server. Each type of form element that can interact with the user is demonstrated by example.

Covers

Chapter Ten

A simple form

A form is a section of a HTML document body that can contain regular content together with a number of "controls" which may be modified by the user.

Typical controls include text inputs and radio buttons.

The modified form can be submitted to the server where the forms control input will be processed.

All form content is contained in **<form> </form>** tags.

The **<form>** tag must have an **action** attribute that specifies the location of a form handler to process the form data when the form is submitted to the server.

Often the form handler will be a CGI script like the address assigned to the **action** attribute in this simple form:

form.html

```
<body>
<form action="http://domain/formhandler.cgi">
<p>
First name: <input type="text" name="firstname"> <br>
Last name: <input type="text" name="lastname"> <br>
<input type="radio" name="sex" value="Male">Male
<input type="radio" name="sex" value="Female">Female
<input type="submit" value="Submit">
</p>
</form>
</body>
```

A form must also provide a means for the user to submit the form data.

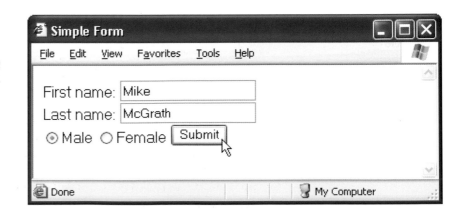

Submission information

For more on form-handling with CGI scripts refer to "Perl in easy steps".

The HTML **<form>** tag has several attributes that may be used to provide information regarding form submission.

An attribute named **method** can specify the type of form submission as either **"get"** or **"post"**. If unspecified the default method is **"get"** although **"post"** is preferred for submissions to CGI script form handlers.

Each form will automatically submit its data in an encoded format that is acceptable to the server. This default MIME type is **"application/x-www-form-urlencoded"**.

Optionally the encoding type can be specified manually with a **<form>** attribute called **enctype**.

For instance the **enctype** attribute may specify a MIME type to indicate the submission of another file by assigning a value of **"multipart/form-data"**.

Alternatively submissions in plain text format might assign a MIME type of **"text/plain"** to the **enctype** attribute.

Most forms however will use the default encoding so the **enctype** need not be set manually.

All forms should be named by assigning a unique name to the **name** attribute in the **<form>** tag. The given name can then be used by scripts to refer to the form.

The opening **<form>** tag on the opposite page could be amended to name the form as **"myform"** and because it is a submission to a CGI script the **"post"** method is specified:

```
<form name="myform"
    action="http://domain/formhandler.cgi"
     method="post">
```

It is important to understand that all form submissions consist of name/value pairs, so the form handler will receive a name together with an associated value.

All the controls in a HTML form must therefore contain a **name** and **value** attribute to submit to the form handler.

Text inputs

Many form controls use a HTML **<input>** tag with a **type** attribute that specifies the type of that control.

The **<input>** tag does not have any closing tag.

One of the most common controls is the text input that is created with an **<input>** tag and an assigned type of **"text"**.

To make the text input useful to a form handler it must also have a name and a value. These are assigned to the **<input>** **name** and **value** attributes for submission by the form.

*The width of the text input will be set by the browser's interpretation of the **size** attribute value.*

Optionally the width of a text input can be specified by assigning an integer to a **size** attribute of the **<input>** tag.

The example below creates a text input with the **name** of **"txt1"**, a **size** of **"12"** and an initial **value** of **"Enter"**.

A user can change this initial value and the form will submit the input **name** and its final **value** as a name/value pair:

text.html

```
<body>
<form name="myform" method="post"
   action="http://domain/formhandler.cgi">
<p>
<input name="txt1" type="text" value="Enter" size="12">
<br> <input type="submit" value="Submit Form">
</p>
</form>
</body>
```

*Add **onfocus**, **onselect** or **onblur** attributes to call a script from an active text input.*

Password inputs

A user can enter an unlimited number of characters into a text input unless a limit is set with a **maxlength** attribute.

An **<input>** tag's **maxlength** attribute specifies a maximum number of characters that can be entered into an input field.

This may also be used with the **"password"** type of **<input>** which is simply a variation of the regular **"text" type** input.

The only difference is that the password input field displays an asterisk in place of each actual character of the text content, to safeguard against a password being easily visible.

All other attributes that are used in the text input can be used by a password input.

When a form is submitted the password inputs name and actual character content are sent to the form handler.

The example below sets no initial **<input> value** but limits the maximum permitted entry length to 6 characters:

maxlength.html

```
<body>
<form name="myform" method="post"
    action="http://domain/formhandler.cgi">
<p>Enter Password [Max.6] <br>
<input name="pwd1" type="password" maxlength="6">
<input type="submit" value="Submit">
</p>
</form>
</body>
```

A script could advise the user when the maximum entry length had been

exceeded.

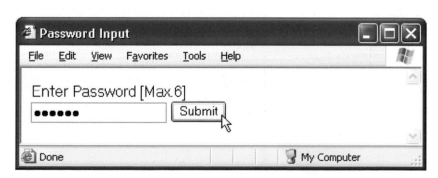

Checkboxes

A **"checkbox" type input** is a HTML form control which the user can choose to select or ignore. If a checkbox has been selected its **name** and associated **value** will be sent to the form handler when the form is submitted.

The CGI script does not receive any data for "chk2" because that checkbox is not selected.

Normally each checkbox will be given a unique name but checkboxes may share a common name to apply multiple values to the same property.

This example below applies two values to the **"chk1"** property and the CGI script outputs all name/value data:

checkbox.html

```
<body>
<form name="myform" method="post"
    action="http://localhost/cgi-bin/showall.cgi">
<p>
<input name="chk1" value="coffee" type="checkbox">Coffee
<input name="chk1" value="cream" type="checkbox">Cream
<input name="chk2" value="sugar" type="checkbox">Sugar
<input type="submit" value="Submit">
</p>
</form>
</body>
```

Add the single word **checked** into the input tag to set the initial selection.

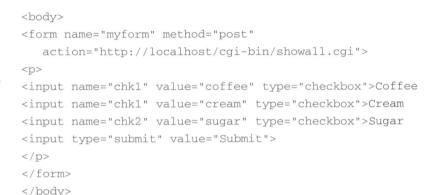

Radio buttons

A **"radio" type input** is normally one of a group of radio buttons that share a common name. Unlike checkboxes, only one button in the group can be selected at any given time. When the form is submitted only the selected radio button's **name** and value are sent.

The name and value of the initially selected radio button will always be submitted unless the user selects a different button.

A radio button group must always have one button selected. The button to be initially selected can be specified by adding the single word **checked** into its **<input>** tag.

This example submits the selected button name/value to the CGI script form handler which outputs the data received:

radio.html

```
<body>
<form name="myform" method="post"
    action="http://localhost/cgi-bin/showall.cgi">
<p>
<input name="Pop" value="Lemon" type="radio">Lemonade
<input name="Pop" value="Cola" type="radio" checked>Cola
<input name="Pop" value="Orange" type="radio">Orangeade
<input type="submit" value="Submit">
</p>
</form>
</body>
```

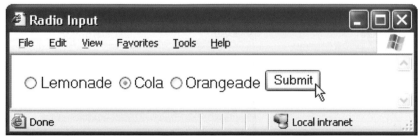

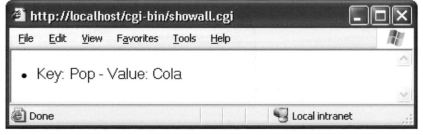

File inputs

A **"file" type input** may select a file for upload with the creation of a special form control.

The control includes a browse facility that allows the user to select an alternative file from a selection dialog.

When the file is selected its path is displayed in a text field which can also be used to type the path of a chosen file.

Also a default file name can be specified with the **value** attribute of the **<input>** tag.

Using this type of input the **<form>** tag should specify the MIME type as **"multipart/form-data"** with its **enctype** attribute to denote that the submission includes a file.

This example creates a file selection input and illustrates a user-selected file ready for submission to the server:

file.html

The browser may not display the initial file value in the text field.

```
<body>
<form name="myform" enctype="multipart/formdata"
    method="post" action="http://domain/handler.cgi">
<p>
Please select a file for upload...<br>
<input name="fselect" type="file" value="C:\this.file">
<br> <input type="submit" value="Click To Upload">
</p>
</form>
</body>
```

Hidden inputs

A **"hidden" type input** does not create any visible form control but is used to store data for submission.

This is particularly useful for scripts to maintain user data when generating a HTML document.

When the form is subsequently submitted the original user data is again sent to the server.

The example below has a **readonly "text" type input** plus a **"hidden" type input** and will submit both name/value pairs:

hidden.html

*Add the word **readonly** to text inputs to prevent the user changing the value of the text field.*

```
<body>
<form name="myform" method="post"
    action="http://localhost/cgi-bin/showall.cgi">
<p>
<input name="txt1" type="text" value="Look no hands"
readonly>
<input name="hid1" type="hidden" value="Hidden Hands">
<input type="submit" value="Submit">
</p>
</form>
</body>
```

Push buttons

The **"button" type** of **<input>** creates a push button control that is typically used to run a script function.

A button should have a **name** and **value** but neither of these are generally used when the form is submitted to the server.

Whatever is assigned to the **<input>** tags **value** attribute will be displayed on the button face as its label.

It is the **<input>** tag's **onclick** attribute that is used to execute a script function when the user pushes that button.

The script function will often be contained in a script block within the document **head** section or in a linked script file.

In the example below some script code is assigned "in-line" to the **onclick** attribute to run when the button is pushed.

This code assigns the browser name to a **text input value**:

button.html

Script functions will not run if the browser does not support the scripting language or it is disabled in user preferences.

```
<body>
<form name="myform" method="post"
      action="http://localhost/cgi-bin/showall.cgi">
<p>
<input name="txt1" type="text" size="28"> <br>
<input name="btn1" type="button" value="Show Browser"
       onclick="this.form.txt1.value=navigator.appName">
<input type="submit" value="Submit">
</p>
</form>
</body>
```

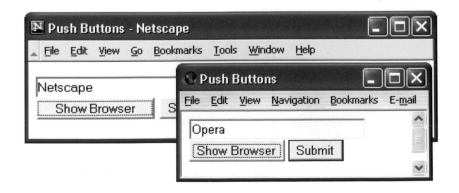

Reset buttons

A **"reset" type** button can be added to a form to allow the user to return all the form values to their original state.

The reset button is created by assigning **"reset"** to the **<input>** tags **type** attribute.

In this example the reset button returns the text input value to its initial value of an empty string:

reset.html

*An **onreset** attribute can be added to the **<form>** tag to run a script whenever a form is reset.*

```
<body>
<form name="myform" method="post"
    action="http://localhost/cgi-bin/showall.cgi">
<p>
<input name="txt1" type="text" size="28" value="">
<br>
<input name="rst1" type="reset" value="Reset">
<input type="submit" value="Submit">
</p>
</form>
</body>
```

Submit buttons

The **"submit" input type** creates a button that the user can push to send the form data to the server. The form controls **name** and **value** data is typically submitted to a CGI script form handler as name/value pairs.

An **onsubmit** attribute can be added to the **<form>** tag to assign a script that will run when the form is submitted. The script will be executed immediately before the form is submitted so it can make any last minute checks.

This example uses the **onsubmit** attribute to round down floating point values to whole integers in the text input:

onsubmit.html

A single form may contain multiple submit buttons.

```
<body>
<form name="myform" method="post"
action="http://localhost/cgi-bin/showall.cgi"
onsubmit="myform.txt1.value=Math.floor(myform.txt1.value)">
<p>
<input name="txt1" type="text" value="3.142">
<input type="submit" value="Submit">
</p>
</form>
</body>
```

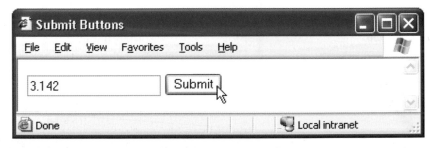

Image submit button

The **"image" input type** can create a graphical submit button.

This also requires a **src** attribute to specify the location of the button image and an **alt** attribute to specify alternative text for browsers that do not display images.

When the form is submitted the x and y coordinates where the image was clicked are also sent to the server as seen here:

imgbutton.html

```
<body>
<form name="myform" method="post"
    action="http://localhost/cgi-bin/showall.cgi">
<p>
<input name="txt1" type="text" value="HTML is Fun">
<input type="image" src="send.gif" alt="Submit Button">
</p>
</form>
</body>
```

The submitted coordinates are the position across the image – not the position across the page.

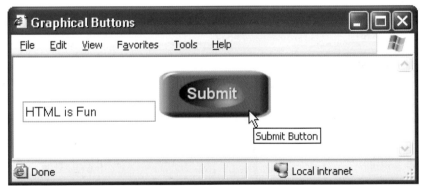

Buttons with graphics

The HTML 4 **<button>** **</button>** tags provide another way to feature a push button in a document. Content between the tags is displayed on the button face and can include text and images.

This example illustrates how the **<button>** tags can be used to make attractive submit, reset and button types:

logobutton.html

```
<body>
<form name="myform" method="post"
    action="http://localhost/cgi-bin/showall.cgi">
<p>
<button name="btn1" value="hi" type="button"
        onclick="alert('Hi!')">
<img src="lilguy.gif" alt="Hi">Welcome</button>
</p>
<hr>
<p>
<button name="btn2" value="submit" type="submit">
<img src="submit.gif" alt="Submit">Submit</button>
 
<button name="btn3" type="reset">
<img src="reset.gif" alt="Reset">Cancel</button>
</p>
</form>
</body>
```

*These buttons work just like buttons created with **<input>** but can add images onto the button face.*

This tag is not implemented in Netscape browsers earlier than version 6.

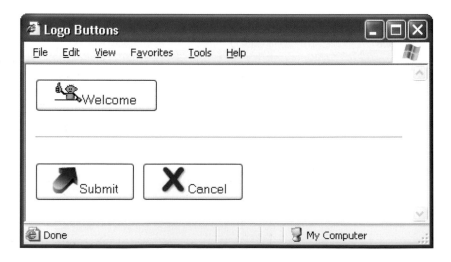

Using labels

Text can be associated with a form control by adding the **<label>** and **</label>** tags to the document.

This tag can have a **for** attribute to assign a controls identity or may surround the control and the associated text.

This example uses both methods to illustrate how the label text can be emphasized with a stylesheet rule:

labels.html

```
<head>
<title>Labels</title>
<style type="text/css">
label {background-color:yellow; color:purple }
</style>
</head>

<body>
<form name="myform" method="post"
    action="http://localhost/cgi-bin/showall.cgi">
<p>Please
<label for="color">enter a color</label> of choice<br>
<input name="color" type="text" id="color"> <br>then
<label>enter a size<br><input type="text" name="size">
</label>
<input type="submit" value="Submit">
</p>
</form>
</body>
```

Using the second method <label> tags should only surround the text and a single control.

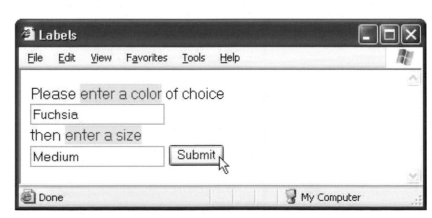

Text areas

The **<textarea>** and **</textarea>** tags are used to create multi-line text input fields in HTML documents. They must always contain both **rows** and **cols** attributes to specify the width and height of the text input field. Also a **name** attribute will be assigned a given name.

Unlike a regular text input a **<textarea>** has no **value** attribute. Instead it takes any text content between its tags to be its associated value, as seen in the example below:

textarea.html

```
<body>
<form name="myform" method="post"
    action="http://localhost/cgi-bin/showall.cgi">
<p>
<textarea name="tar1" rows="3" cols="25">
You may change the text in this area.</textarea>
<input type="submit" value="Submit">
</p>
</form>
</body>
```

Text areas will automatically have a scroll bar to accommodate long content.

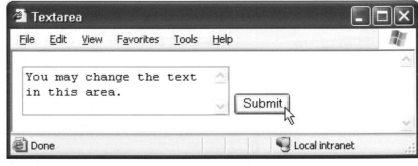

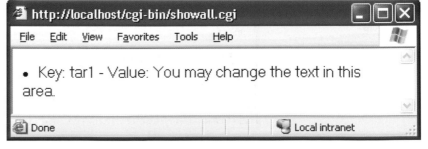

Tab order

A tab key can be used to navigate through the hyperlinks and form controls in a HTML document, normally following the order in which they appear in the document.

A special tab order can be determined by adding a **tabindex** attribute to any of the tags **<a>**, **<area>**, **<button>**, **<input>**, **<object>**, **<select>** or **<textarea>**.

These are assigned unique integer values to set the tab order.

Any of the form controls in the above list of tags can be disabled by adding the single word **disabled** into its tag.

Disabled form controls cannot receive input, are not submitted with the form and are ignored in the tab order.

This example has a special tab order and a disabled control:

tab.html

```
<body>
<form name="myform" method="post"
      action="http://localhost/cgi-bin/showall.cgi">
<p>
<input type="text" size="1" tabindex="5">
<input type="text" size="1" tabindex="4" disabled>
<input type="text" size="1" tabindex="3">
<input type="text" size="1" tabindex="2">
<input type="submit" value="Submit" tabindex="1">
</p>
</form>
</body>
```

Controls that are disabled may appear "grayed-out" in some browsers.

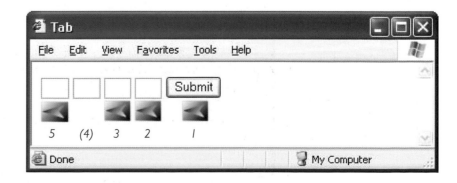

Selection menus

The **<select>** and **</select>** tags create a selection menu from which the user may select a listed option.

The **<select>** tags should assign a given name to a **name** attribute and should surround the list of options.

Text describing each option is contained between **<option>** **</option>** tags and each one must have a **value** attribute.

Add *size="3"* to this *<select>* tag to make the menu fixed.

When the form is submitted the **<select>** name and the **<option>** value make up the submitted name/value pair.

The select menu generally appears as a drop-down list unless a **size** attribute is added to the **<select>** tag to set a height.

The example below illustrates a selection menu and adds the single word **selected** to initially select one of the options:

select.html

```
<body>
<form name="myform" method="post"
    action="http://localhost/cgi-bin/showall.cgi"> <p>
<select name="myselect">
<option value="1st">First Choice</option>
<option value="2nd" selected>Second Choice</option>
<option value="3rd">Third Choice</option>
</select>
<input type="submit" value="Submit"> </p>
</form>
</body>
```

Add an **onchange** attribute in the **<select>** tag to call a script function upon selection.

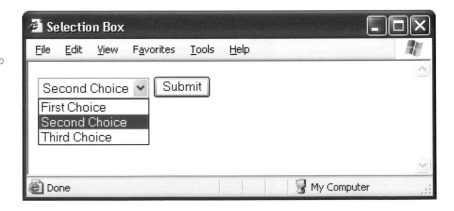

Grouping menus

Select menu options may be grouped together with the **\<optgroup\>** and **\</optgroup\>** tags.

A name for each group can be assigned to a **label** attribute inside its **\<optgroup\>** tag.

The example below displays the name given to each option group in the fixed-height select menu:

group.html

```
<body>
<form name="myform" method="post"
    action="http://localhost/cgi-bin/showall.cgi">
<p>
<select name="myselect" size="6">
<optgroup label="Group 1">
<option value="1,1st">First Choice</option>
<option value="1,2nd">Second Choice</option>
</optgroup>
<optgroup label="Group 2">
<option value="2,1st">First Choice</option>
<option value="2,2nd">Second Choice</option>
</optgroup>
</select>
<input type="submit" value="Submit">
</p>
</form>
</body>
```

Browsers that do not support **\<optgroup\>** *will still display the select menu –*
without the group labels.

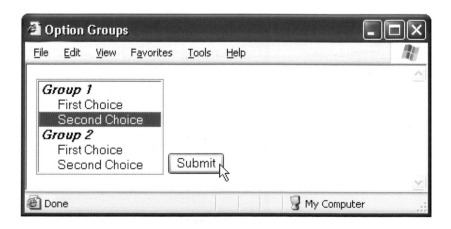

Grouping form fields

Associated form input fields can be grouped into "fieldsets" which the browser may display in a manner that makes their association apparent to the user.

The **<fieldset> </fieldset>** tags are used to contain the associated inputs. The fieldset may also display a group name defined between **<legend> </legend>** tags.

This example illustrates two fieldsets and legends:

fieldset.html

Browsers may display fieldsets in a variety of different ways.

```
<body>
<form name="myform" method="post"
   action="http://localhost/cgi-bin/showall.cgi">
 <fieldset> <legend>Select Color</legend>
 <input type="radio" name="colr" value="red" checked>Red
 <input type="radio" name="colr" value="grn">Green
 <input type="radio" name="colr" value="blu">Blue
 </fieldset>
 <fieldset> <legend>Select Size</legend>
 <input type="radio" name="size" value="s">Small
 <input type="radio" name="size" value="m">Medium
 <input type="radio" name="size" value="l" checked>Large
 </fieldset>
<p> <input type="submit" value="Submit"> </p>
</form>
</body>
```

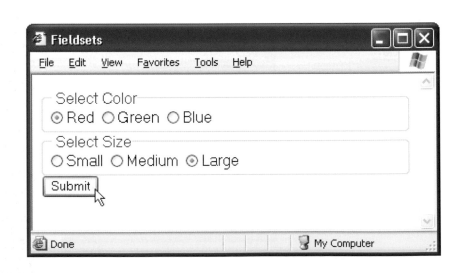

Borders and margins

This chapter explains the components comprising blocks of HTML document content. Examples demonstrate how style rules can be used to manipulate each component.

Covers

Chapter Eleven

The content box

Each block of document content is placed onto the page in an invisible content box.

The content box has three properties that may optionally specify how the block of content appears.

Content box properties have a top, bottom, left and right part that can be addressed individually.

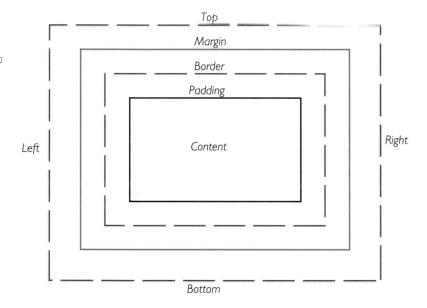

A **padding** property defines the edges of the content box. With a padding width of zero the content box edges are identical to the contained content edges. The content box edges extend as the padding width is increased.

A **border** property defines the width of the area immediately surrounding the content box. With a border width of zero the border edges remain identical to the content box edges. The border edges extend as the border width is increased.

A **margin** property defines the width of the area that immediately surrounds the border edges. With a margin width of zero the margin edges remain identical to the border edges. The margin edges extend as the margin width is increased.

Background and border color

To create a border around a block of content it is necessary to specify its border properties for color, width and style.

The stylesheet **border-color** property will specify the color of the entire content box border.

Similarly its width can be specified with a **border-width** property and style of border with a **border-style** property.

Individual border colors could have also been set using the properties border-left-color and border-right-color.

The example below initially sets all content box borders to black with a width of 25 pixels and drawn in a solid style.

A **background-color** property is assigned a recognized color name to set a background color for the content box.

Top and bottom borders are assigned individual colors that supersede the general border color for just those borders.

border.html

```
<head>
<title>Background &amp; Border Color</title>
<style type="text/css">
p { border-color:purple; border-width:25px;
    border-style:solid; background-color:yellow;
    border-top-color:lime; border-bottom-color:lime }
</style>
</head>

<body>
<p>Content</p>
</body>
```

Remember to set a width and style as well as the color.

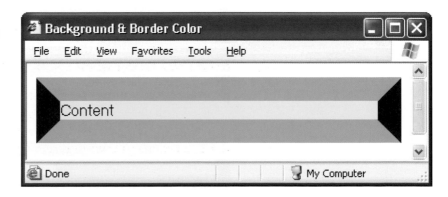

Border style

The style for all four borders around a content box may be set collectively with the style sheet **border-style** property.

Or individually they can be specified with the properties **border-style-top**, **border-style-bottom**, **border-style-left** and **border-style-right**.

The illustration below shows the available border styles and how each border style might be displayed by the browser:

In order to hide a border, set its style property to none.

Remember to set a width and color as well as the style.

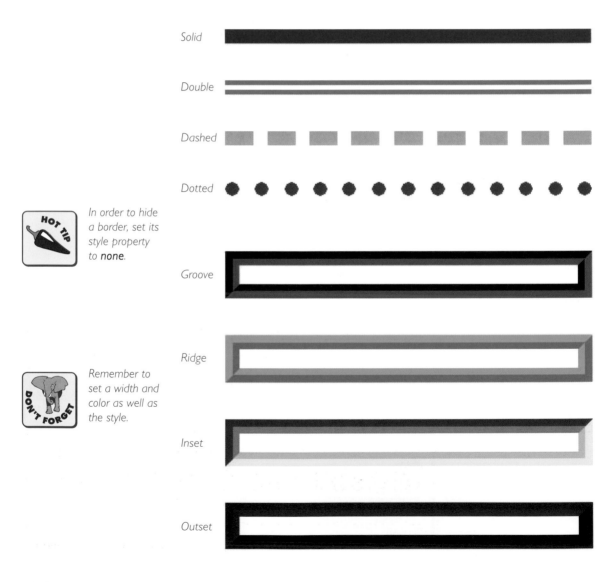

Solid

Double

Dashed

Dotted

Groove

Ridge

Inset

Outset

Border width

The width of all four borders around a content box may be set collectively with the stylesheet **border-width** property.

Or individually they can be specified with the properties **border-width-top**, **border-width-bottom**, **border-width-left** and **border-width-right**.

*Border-width properties may alternatively have general width values of **thin**, **medium** or **thick**.*

The example below sets a uniform width for the lime border around the first paragraph drawn in a **double** style.

Individual border widths are specified for the fuchsia border around the second paragraph which also has a **double** style:

borderwidth.html

```
<head>
<title>Border Width</title>
<style type="text/css">
#p1 {border-color:lime; border-style:ridge;
    border-width:10px }
#p2 {border-color:fuchsia; border-style:ridge;
     border-width:10px;
       border-top-width:3px; border-bottom-width:20px }
</style>
</head>

<body>
<p id="p1">Content</p><p id="p2">Content</p>
</body>
```

Remember to set a color and style as well as the width.

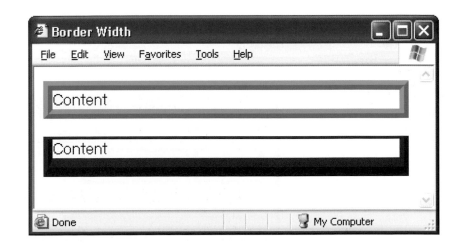

Border shorthand

A single style sheet property called **border** may alternatively specify all the required rules to set a border.

This shorthand version can only be used when all four borders in a content box are to have the same appearance.

The **border** property collectively specifies values for a border's width, style and color with the following syntax:

```
border: border-width border-style border-color ;
```

In the example below the border around the first content box is set with individual properties.

The second content box border appears identical to the first one but is set using the shorthand **border** version:

bordershort.html

```
<head>
<title>Border Shorthand</title>
<style type="text/css">
#s1 {border-width:5px; border-style:outset;
        border-color:lime; padding:5px }
#s2 {border:5px outset fuchsia; padding:5px }
</style>
</head>

<body>
<p>
<span id="s1">Content</span>
<span id="s2">More Content</span>
</p>
</body>
```

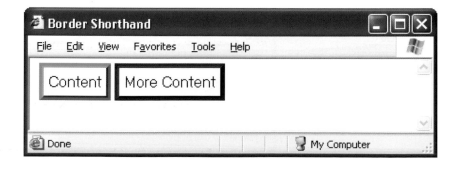

Add padding

The padding area around the actual content in a content box can be specified with a **padding** stylesheet property. This sets a general padding width surrounding the contained content at top, bottom, left and right.

Individual padding widths can be set with stylesheet properties of **padding-top**, **padding-bottom**, **padding-left** and **padding-right**.

This example applies overall padding in the first paragraph and top padding over the content in the second paragraph:

padding.html

The HTML 4 specification requires that the "px" suffix should always follow the numeric value when assigning pixel sizes.

```
<head>
<title>Padding</title>
<style type="text/css">
p { border-color:purple; border-width:thick;
    border-style:solid; background color:yellow }
#p1 { padding:20px }
#p2 { padding-top:40px }
</style>
</head>

<body>
<p id="p1">Content</p> <p id="p2">Content</p>
</body>
```

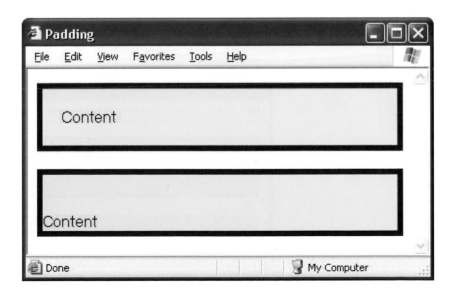

Relative padding

Padding areas in a content box can alternatively be specified relative to other aspects of the document. They may be specified as a percentage of the block in which they are contained or relative to the current size of font.

This example applies padding twice the width of the current font then 60% of the surrounding **\<div\>** element:

relpadding.html

```
<head>
<title>Relative Padding</title>
<style type="text/css">
div { width:100% }
p { border-color:black; border-width:thin;
    border-style:solid; padding-left:2em }
#p1 { font-size:8pt; background-color:yellow }
#p2 { font-size:14pt; background-color:lime }
#p3 { padding-left:60%; background-color:fuchsia }
</style>
</head>
```

The "em" suffix is a unit value equivalent to the size of the current font.

```
<body>
<div>
<p id="p1">Content</p>
<p id="p2">Content</p>
<p id="p3">Content</p>
</div>
</body>
```

Percentages are not relative to the content box itself but to the block that contains the content box.

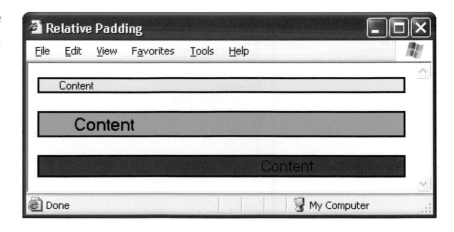

Padding shorthand

A single stylesheet property called **padding** may alternatively specify all the padding areas of a content box. The **padding** property may collectively specify values for top, right, bottom and left padding areas.

If only one value is specified it applies to all four sides.

*Padding rules will be added **in order** to the top, right, bottom and left padding areas.*

If two values are specified the first applies to top and bottom sides and the second applies to left and right sides.

If three values are specified the first applies to the top side, the second applies to both left and right sides and the third applies to the bottom side.

If four values are specified they apply, in sequence, to the padding areas on the top, right, bottom and left sides.

In this example the **border** shorthand property creates borders and the **padding** shorthand property adds padding:

paddingshort.html

Notice that comments within stylesheets must begin with /* and end with */ – like comments in JavaScript.

```
<head>
<title>Padding Shorthand</title>
<style type="text/css">
span{ border:inset fuchsia 6px;background-color:yellow }
/* pad top, right, bottom, left */
#s1 { padding: 5px 20px 10px 100px }
</style>
</head>

<body> <p>      <span id="s1">Content</span>
                <span id="s2">Content</span>        </p>
</body>
```

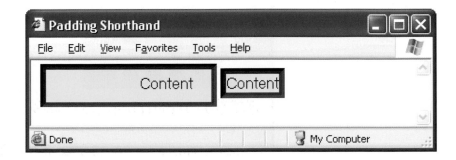

Set margins

Margin areas may be specified with the **margin** stylesheet property that sets all block margins to the assigned size.

Individual margins can be set using stylesheet properties of **margin-top**, **margin-bottom**, **margin-left** and **margin-right**.

The example below sets the default body margins to zero for a **<div>** element to display at the extreme top left of a page. A nested **<div>** element has its top, left and right margins set to be 20 pixels from the edge of the containing **<div>** element:

margins.html

Margins may be interpreted differently by each browser.

```
<head>
<title>Margins</title>
<style type="text/css">
body { margin:0px }
#d1 { background-color:lime; margin:0px;
      width:200px; height:75px }
#d2 { background-color:yellow; padding:3px;
      border-width:8px; border-style:dashed;
      border-color:purple; margin-top:20px;
      margin-left:20px; margin-right:20px }
</style>
</head>

<body>
<div id="d1">
    <div id="d2"> <span>Content</span> </div>
</div>
</body>
```

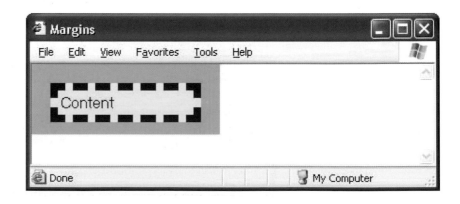

Margin shorthand

A single stylesheet property called **margin** may alternatively specify all the margin areas of a content box.

The **margin** property may collectively specify values for top, right, bottom and left margin areas. If only one value is specified it applies to all four sides.

If two values are specified the first applies to top and bottom sides and the second applies to left and right sides.

If three values are specified the first applies to the top side, the second applies to both left and right sides and the third applies to the bottom side.

If four values are specified they apply, in sequence, to the margin areas on the top, right, bottom and left sides.

In this example the **border** shorthand property creates borders, the **padding** shorthand property adds padding and the **margin** shorthand property sets margins:

marginshort.html

Notice that the right margin value forces the second content box away right.

```
<head>
<title>Margin Shorthand</title>
<style type="text/css">
span { border:double purple 5px; background-color:lime }
#s1  { padding:5px; margin:5px 70px 5px 30px }
</style>
</head>

<body> <p>      <span id="s1">Content</span>
                <span id="s2">Content</span>      </p>
</body>
```

Putting it together

This fuller example uses some of the border, margin, padding and background color properties seen in this chapter:

together.html

```
<head>
<title>Putting It Together</title>
<style type="text/css">
body { border:ridge 30px fuchsia; background-color:lime}
p    { border:dotted 5px purple; padding:10px;
       background-color:yellow; margin:20px }
h3   { color:red }
</style>
</head>

<body>
<h3>Borders Are Fun...</h3>
<p>If they are used<br>in sensible moderation.</p>
</body>
```

Notice here how Internet Explorer moves the scroll bar inside the content box border – other browsers may be different.

Positioning content boxes

This chapter explains the system of coordinates used to reference specific points in a HTML document. There are examples demonstrating how to precisely place document content with style sheet rules.

Covers

Chapter Twelve

XYZ coordinates

Physical position of content in a display window can be referred to using coordinates called "X", "Y" and "Z".

The X coordinate specifies the distance in pixels from the extreme left edge of the window.

The Y coordinate specifies the distance in pixels from the extreme top edge of the window.

The Z coordinate specifies the stacked position by index number of layers above the bottom window level:

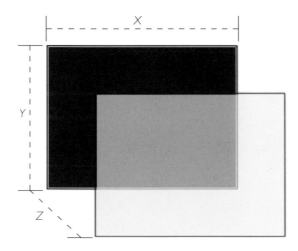

To differentiate the coordinates remember that "a cross" (X) means "across".

The X coordinate at the left edge of the window is zero and the Y coordinate at the top edge of the window is also zero.

A position where X=50 and Y=30 would pinpoint a location 50 pixels from the left edge and 30 pixels from the top edge.

The Z coordinate of the bottom window level has an index value of zero. Layers may be placed over this level, like transparent sheets, and are given unique Z-index values.

A window may have many layers but the top layer will always have the highest Z-index value. Each successive layer below that will have a decreasingly lower Z-index value.

Absolute positioning

The position of document content boxes can be controlled with a style property called **position**.

To determine a precise location the **position** property should be set as **absolute**.

The Y coordinate of the content box is then specified by assigning a pixel value to a style property called **top**. This sets the top edge of the content box at the given distance from the top of the window, or outer containing block.

Similarly the X coordinate of the content box is specified by assigning a pixel value to a style property called **left**. This sets the left edge of the content block at the given distance from the left of the window, or outer containing block.

This example absolutely positions three content boxes:

absolute.html

*If the content box is nested in a containing block its **top** and **left** positions are set relative to that block's edges – not to those of the entire window.*

```
<head>
<title>Absolute Positioning</title>
<style type="text/css">
div { background-color:yellow; width:100px }
#d1 { position:absolute; top:0px; left:0px; width:auto }
#d2 { position:absolute; top:30px; left:80px }
#d3 { position:absolute; top:10px; left:170px }
</style>
</head>

<body> <div id="d1"><p>X=0, Y=0</p></div>
       <div id="d2"><p>X=80, Y=30</p></div>
       <div id="d3"><p>X=170, Y=10</p></div>
</body>
```

Absolute Positioning

File Edit View Favorites Tools Help

X=0, Y=0

X=170, Y=10

X=80, Y=30

Done   My Computer

Z-order

Absolute positioning is used to specify the Z-axis stacking order of layers, in addition to setting X and Y coordinates.

The Z-index value is assigned to a style property that is called **z-index** in order to set the layers stacking position.

Layers are positioned in ascending order according to their **z-index** value so that higher layers can overlap those below.

This example sets some general styles for the **<div>** content blocks then positions them absolutely and stacked:

stack.html

```
<head>
<title>Z-Order Positioning</title>
<style type="text/css">
div { border:solid 3px purple; width:100px; height:50;
      background-color:yellow; padding:3px }
#d1 { position:absolute; top:10px; left:40px;
      z-index:10 }
#d2 { position:absolute; top:50px; left:120px;
      z-index:20 }
</style>
</head>

<body>
<div id="d1"><p>Layer 1<br>Z-Index=10</p></div>
<div id="d2"><p>Layer 2<br>Z-Index=20</p></div>
</body>
```

Number layers in increments of 10 – so it's easy to slip other layers in between later if needed.

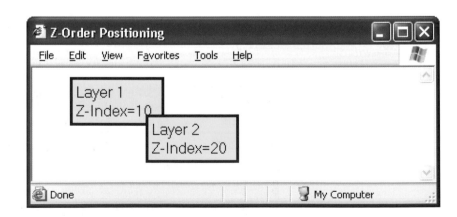

Relative positioning

The style **position** property can be set to **relative** to adjust the position of content boxes relative to the normal flow of other content.

Regular content flow initially lays out the content box position then this can be adjusted by a style **position** rule.

In the example below all content boxes are initially laid out in the regular flow that is indicated by a dotted line.

Style rules then adjust the position of two of the content boxes **relative** to their regular flow position:

relative.html

```
<head>
<title>Relative Positioning</title>
<style type="text/css">
span { width:20; height:20; background-color:purple;
       color:yellow; margin:5px; text-align:center }
.up { position:relative; top:-15px }
.dn { position:relative; top:50px }
</style>
</head>

<body><p>
<span>1</span><span>2</span><span class="up">3</span>
<span>4</span><span>5</span><span class="dn">6</span>
<span>7</span><span>8</span></p>
</body>
```

It is convenient to create a class to specify a **relative** style position rule.

The **text-align** property in this example ensures that each box number appears centrally. See page 159 for more details on this property.

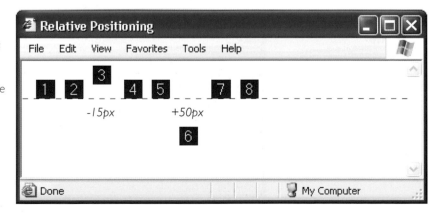

Floating boxes

A content box can be made to the extreme left or right of the current line with the style **float** property. This property can be set to **left** or **right** to move the position of the content box.

Most importantly this allows other content to then flow around that content box.

The example below has a paragraph containing two sentences plus an image content box that is floated to the left of the current line:

float.html

```
<head>
<title>Floating Boxes</title>
<style type="text/css">
#i1 { float:left }
</style>
</head>

<body>
<p>
The <img id="i1" src="lilguy.gif" width="58" height="48"
alt="lilguy">text in this paragraph simply wraps around
the floating box. After the bottom of the floating box
the lines once again start at their normal position.
This is great for illustrating text with small images -
like the one seen here.
</p>
</body>
```

The text wrapping may appear differently on other browsers.

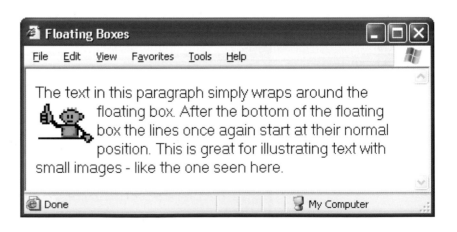

Clear side

Content can be prevented from wrapping around a floating box with the style **clear** property. This can specify that its **left** or **right** side must remain clear and cannot be adjacent to a floating box.

With the example on the facing page the second sentence can be prevented from wrapping around the image content box.

The example below adds a clear style rule to the second sentence ensuring that it appears below the image content box rather than wrapped around it:

clear.html

```
<head>
<title>Clear Side</title>
<style type="text/css">
#i1 { float:left }
#s1 { clear:left }
</style>
</head>
<body>
<p>The <img id="i1" src="lilguy.gif" width="58"
height="48" alt="lilguy"> text in this sentence wraps
around the floating box - just like the example on the
opposite page.<span id="s1">The text in the second
sentence is not allowed to wrap.</span>
</p>
</body>
```

*Content boxes floated **right** would still wrap text that has a **clear:left** side.*

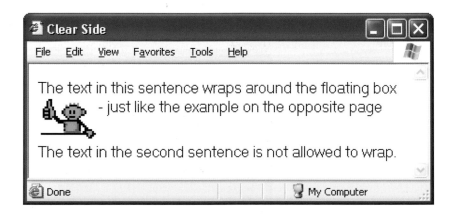

Content box resize

The width and height of a content box is specified with the style **width** and **height** properties. Despite this explicit sizing instruction some browsers will automatically resize the height of the content box if the contained content will not fit the specified height.

This example shows how overflowing content may appear:

resize.html

```
<head>
<title>Content Box Resize</title>
<style type="text/css">
div { border:solid 1px purple; margin:5px;
     width:150px; height:20px }
</style>
</head>

<body> <div>150x20 Pixels</div>
<div>This text will not fit in a box of 150x20 pixels
</div>
</body>
```

Overflow can be created when a browser uses a large font – see chapter 13 for how to control the font size.

Overflow

The style **overflow** property can be used to specify how the browser should handle content that will not fit inside the content box fixed width and fixed height.

Assigning this property a **visible** value allows the browser to display the overflow content outside the content box.

Alternatively the **overflow** property can be set to **hidden** – which will hide any content that will not fit into the content box.

This may make it inaccessible to the user though.

A **scroll** value can be assigned to **overflow** to indicate that the content may overflow and browsers that support content box scrollbars should display them in that box.

Scroll bars handle the overflowing content in this example:

overflow.html

Allow extra space for the scroll bar dimensions when setting the overall content box size.

```
<head>
<title>Handling Overflow</title>
<style type="text/css">
div { border:solid 1px purple; width:150px;
      height:65px; overflow:scroll }
</style>
</head>

<body>
<div>This text will not fit in a box of 150x20 pixels
but the user can scroll down to read it all.</div>
</body>
```

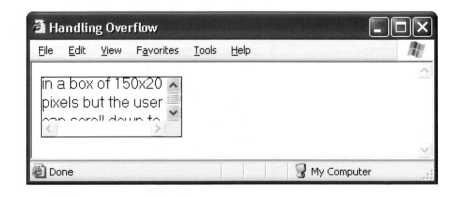

Clipping overflow

The style **clip** property defines a "clipping region" that will be the only visible part of a content box. The clipping region is rectangular and is set as **clip:** *top right bottom left* . The parameters specify the extreme edges of the clipping region in pixel distances across the content box.

In the example below both content boxes contain the same image but the one on the right has been clipped.

clip.html

```
<head>
<title>Clipping</title>
<style type="text/css">
#d1 { position:absolute; top:15px; left:140px;
      clip:rect(0px 110px 80px 30px) }
</style>
</head>

<body><div>
<img src="bart.gif" width="143" height="200" alt="bart">
</div><div id="d1">
<img src="bart.gif" width="143" height="200" alt="bart">
</div>
</body>
```

Other valid measures of distance are "em" units, inches ("in") and centimeters ("cm").

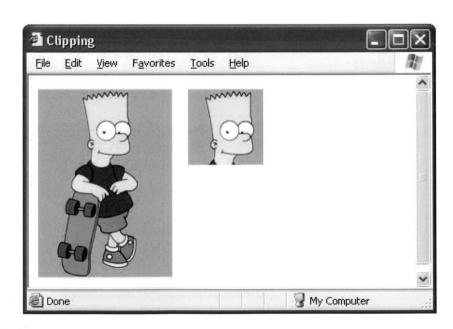

Stylish text

This chapter explores the presentation of text content in a HTML document. There are examples illustrating how to influence the manner of textual display with style rules.

Covers

Chapter Thirteen

Font families

The style **font-family** property allows the HTML document to suggest a generic font to the browser. This overcomes the problem that not all systems can have all fonts and so the generic family will select the most appropriate font that is available on that system.

Valid generic family names are **serif**, **sans-serif**, **cursive**, **fantasy** and **monospace**. The **font-family** property can also suggest a list of fonts by name in a comma-delimited list. Browsers will search for each font in turn. A generic family name should always be suggested as the last alternative in case none of the named fonts are found.

Both **cursive** and **fantasy** font families are decorative while the others are plainer, as seen in this example:

fontfamily.html

Fonts that are members of the **cursive** family usually have characters that appear as handwritten.

```
<head>
<title>Font Families</title>
</head>

<body> <p>
<span style="font-family:serif">Serif - </span>
<span style="font-family:sans-serif">Sans-Serif -</span>
<span style="font-family:monospace">Monospace</span><br>
<span style="font-family:cursive">Cursive - </span>
<span style="font-family:fantasy">Fantasy</span><br>
<span style="font-family:impact,modern,cursive">
            Impact,Modern or Generic Cursive</span>
</p>
</body>
```

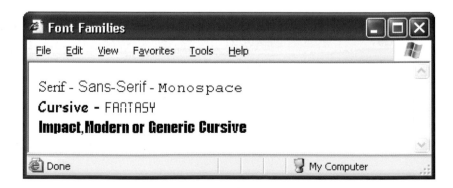

Font size

The size of font to be used by the browser can be specified with the **font-size** style property. Valid values may be either an exact point-size or a size relative to the surrounding font size currently in use. Exact size is set with the suffix "pt", so 12-point is "12pt".

Relative font-size can be specified as **larger** or **smaller**. Alternatively this may be a percentage relative to the surrounding font size. For instance **font-size:200** should set the font size at double that of the surrounding font.

The following example sets a general font size for the paragraph then adds some specific font-size rules illustrating each of the methods given above:

fontsize.html

```
<head>
<title>Font Size</title>
<style type="text/css">
p    { font-size:12pt }
#s1 { font-size:20pt; color:red }
#s2 { font-size:70%; color:green }
#s3 { font-size:larger; color:blue }
</style>
</head>

<body>
<p>This is a 12-point font size<br> but
<span id="s1">this is a 20-point font.</span>
<br>SIZE CAN BE <span id="s2">REDUCED</span> OR
<span id="s3">ENLARGED</span></p>
</body>
```

Set fonts to a specific size in order to avoid overflow from content boxes.

Font style

The appearance of a font can be specified with the property named **font-style** to select upright or slanting characters. If unspecified the default font style is to upright characters.

Setting the **font-style** property to **italic** will display the text in an italicized font with slanting characters. A font style of **oblique** will also generally display as italics. If the general font style in use is italicized the **font-style** property can specify **normal** to display upright text.

This example illustrates both **normal** and **italic** font styles:

fontstyle.html

```
<head>
<title>Font Style</title>
<style type="text/css">
#s1 { font-style:italic; color:red }
#s2 { font-style:normal }
#p2 { font-style:italic; color:blue }
</style>
</head>

<body>
<p id="p1">This paragraph uses default styling but
<span id="s1">italic style</span> can be applied.</p>
<p id="p2">This paragraph uses italic styling but
<span id="s2"> normal style</span> can be applied.</p>
</body>
```

*An **oblique** font style may electronically generate an italic font by slanting a normal font.*

Font weight

The preferred boldness of text can be set with the style **font-weight** property. Simply assigning a value of **bold** will display the text in a bold font. Alternatively the specifications allow for the weight to be specified numerically. This numeric range starts at 100 for lightest and goes up to the boldest at 900, by steps of 100. Normally weighted text is around 500 in the range.

The example below sets a piece of bold text then illustrates the effect of adding font weight from normal to boldest:

fontweight.html

```
<head>
<title>Font Weight</title>
<style type="text/css">
.heavy { font-weight:bold }
#s5 { font-weight:500; color:red }
#s6 { font-weight:600; color:green }
#s7 { font-weight:700; color:blue }
#s8 { font-weight:800; color:purple }
#s9 { font-weight:900; color:orange }
p   { font-size:20pt }
</style>
</head>

<body>
<p>Here is some <span class="heavy">bold</span>text.<br>
<span id="s5"> 500</span><span id="s6"> 600</span>
<span id="s7"> 700</span><span id="s8"> 800</span>
<span id="s9"> 900</span> </p>
</body>
```

Setting lighter font-weights of below 500 seldom changes the appearance.

Font variant

The style **font-variant** property may be used to display text content in small capitals. When assigned a value of **small-caps** the property suggests that the browser should attempt to capitalize the text in a smaller font than the one in current use.

The example below illustrates the results of specifying a **font-variant** of **small-caps** in three different browsers:

fontvariant.html

```
<head>
<title>Font Variant</title>
<style type="text/css">
p    { font-size:16pt }
span { font-variant:small-caps; color:orange }
</style>
</head>

<body>
<p>The <span>small caps</span> font variant.</p>
</body>
```

Some browsers may just capitalize the text for this style property – as seen in this example with Internet Explorer.

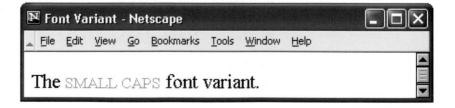

Line height

The style **line-height** property can specify line spacing. The height can be specified as a font point size or as a percentage of the font size in general use by the text. For instance, with a font-size of 12pt setting the line height at 300% would create a line spacing of 36pt.

In the example below the general font size is 12pt and the **line-height** is set at 36pt. Consequently the browser will add extra space over each line of general text.

When the larger 36pt text is encountered an equivalent amount of extra space is added over it and the entire line:

lineheight.html

```
<head>
<title>Line Height</title>
<style type="text/css">
p    { font-size:12pt;line-height:300% }
span { font-size:36pt; color:red }
</style>
</head>
```

When text has more than one font size the browser will calculate a line height from the tallest font.

```
<body> <p>General font size in this paragraph is 12pt.
<br>But here is some<span> 36pt </span> text.<br>
All line heights are also specified as 36pt.</p>
</body>
```

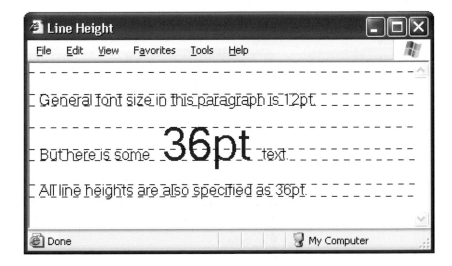

Font shorthand

All the font style properties described earlier in this chapter can be specified together with the **font** property. Each required property is specified in a list like this:

```
font: style variant weight size family;
```

Any of the properties above may be omitted from the list but any included should appear in the given sequential order.

The example below uses the **font** shorthand property to apply font style rules to a tag, an id and a class:

fontshort.html

```
<head>
<title>Font Shorthand</title>
<style type="text/css">
p    { font:12pt serif }
#s1 { font:bold 28pt; color:red }
span.doric { font:italic bold 16pt }
</style>
</head>

<body>
<p>The main attraction of Gortys is the
<br><span id="s1">Code of Laws</span>
<br>These were carved on massive blocks of stone by the
<span class="doric">Dorians</span> </p>
</body>
```

*Specific fonts must still be set with the **font-family** property.*

Some browsers may not support font shorthand – it is safer to set individual font properties.

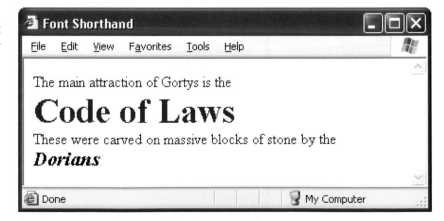

Text and content alignment

The style **text-align** property is used to align text in a content box as either **left**, **right** or **center**. It usefully also aligns any other content such as images.

The example below aligns text in three **\<div\>** content boxes together and illustrates a centered image:

textalign.html

```
<head>
<title>Text Align</title>
<style type="text/css">
div { border:1px solid silver; padding:5px; margin:5px }
#d1 { text-align:left }
#d2 { text-align:right }
#d3 { text-align:center }
</style>
</head>

<body>
<div id="d1">text-align is "left"</div>
<div id="d2">text-align is "right"</div>
<div id="d3">text-align is "center"<br>
<img src="lilguy.gif" width="29" height="24"
    alt="lilguy">
</div>
</body>
```

The **text-align** style property is used with **center** to replace the old HTML **\<center\>** tag.

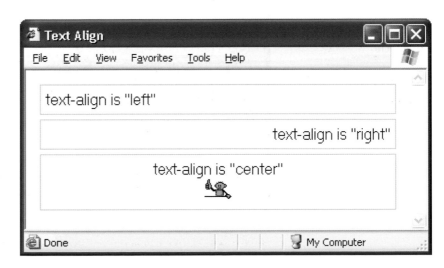

Text decoration

The style **text-decoration** property may add features to text with **underline**, **overline** and **line-through** values. It may also specify **blink** to flash text but this may not be supported in all browsers. Blinking text can be extremely annoying and is best avoided.

In this example the **text-decoration** properties create text with **underline**, **overline** and **line-through**:

decor.html

```
<head>
<title>Text Decoration</title>
<style type="text/css">
div { border:1px solid silver; padding:5px; margin:5px }
#d1 { text-decoration:underline }
#d2 { text-decoration:line-through }
#d3 { text-decoration:overline }
</style>
</head>

<body>
<div id="d1">This is underlined text.</div>
<div id="d2">This text has a line through.</div>
<div id="d3">This text is overlined.</div>
</body>
```

*Text decoration **underline** is used in place of the old HTML **<u>** tag.*

*Text decoration **line-through** is used in place of old HTML **<strike>** tags.*

Indenting text

Traditionally paragraphs have their first line of text indented in order to make the overall flow of text more acceptable. In HTML the style **text-indent** property can specify the amount to indent the first line of text in a content block. The value may be either a fixed amount, like 10 pixels, or a percentage of the width of the containing box.

This example uses the **em** font size units to specify how much the start of each paragraph should be indented:

indent.html

```
<head>
<title>Text Indent</title>
<style type="text/css">
p { text-indent:2em }
</style>
</head>

<body>
<p>One of the best adventures of Crete is a visit to the
Gorge of Samaria.</p>
<p>It is reputed to be the longest gorge in Europe and
may take anywhere between four to seven hours to walk
through.</p>
</body>
```

Specify a negative value to "outdent" the first line of content blocks.

Letter spacing

Extra space can be added between each character with the style **letter-spacing** property. This property can specify a length that is to be added to the normal text spacing between characters.

This may be a fixed distance expressed as pixels like "10px". Alternatively the extra space can be expressed as a distance relative to the font size by using an **em** unit like "1em".

In the example below the first **<span>** adds extra spacing of "1em" and the second **<span>** adds extra spacing of "10px":

lspacing.html

*Use **em** units in preference to pixels to display the text spacing appropriate to the text size.*

```
<head>
<title>Letter Spacing</title>
<style type="text/css">
p   { font-size:20pt }
#s1 { letter-spacing:1em; color:red }
#s2 { letter-spacing:10px; color:blue }
</style>
</head>

<body>
<p>Added <span id="s1">SPACE</span><br>
and <span id="s2">MORE</span> space.</p>
</body>
```

Word spacing

Spaces can be added to the normal spacing between words of text with the style **word-spacing** property. This works like the **letter-spacing** property shown on the facing page but may not be implemented in all browsers.

This example adds a value of "1em" to the default spacing:

wspacing.html

```
<head>
<title>Word Spacing</title>
<style type="text/css">
p    { font-size:14pt }
span { word-spacing:1em }
</style>
</head>

<body>
<p>This is <span>spaced out</span> text.</p>
</body>
```

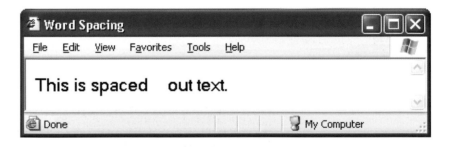

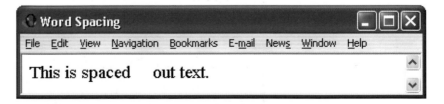

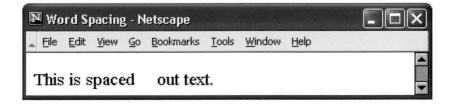

Text direction

The direction of text flow can be controlled with the HTML 4 **<bdo> </bdo>** tags. Its **dir** attribute can specify **"ltr"** for normal left-to-right direction or **"rtl"** for right-to-left text direction. This is useful with languages that run right-to-left where it is advisable for the whole text block to be contained in **<pre> </pre>** tags to conserve spacing and line breaks.

Languages are specified with the **lang** attribute which recognizes special two letter codes for each language.

Two-letter codes include **"en"** (English), **"fr"** (French), **"de"** (German), **"it"** (Italian), **"nl"** (Dutch), **"es"** (Spanish), **"el"** (Greek), **"pt"** (Portugese), **"ar"** (Arabic), **"he"** Hebrew, **"ru"** Russian, **"zh"** (Chinese), **"ja"** (Japanese) and **"hi"** (Hindi).

This example displays Hebrew text correctly as right-to-left:

direction.html

```
<head>
<meta http-equiv="Content-Language" content="en">
<meta http-equiv="Content-Type"
      content="text/html; charset=utf-8">
<title>BiDirectional Order</title>
<style type="text/css">
bdo { font-family: HebrewUniversal; font-size:20pt }
</style>
</head>
```

The examples on these two pages need the HebrewUniversal font installed.

```
<body>
<pre>Hello and<bdo dir="rtl" lang="he" id="bdo2">
שלום </bdo> from Israel.</pre>
</body>
```

Right-to-left style

The text direction in a browser is normally left-to-right but can be changed with the style **unicode-bidi** property. Setting this to **override** will allow the direction to be determined by the style **direction** property as **rtl** or **ltr**.

This starts the entire text content at the right-hand side of the display area and is more suitable for larger sections of text in languages written right-to-left.

In the example below the normal text direction is changed to right-to-left for the entire second paragraph:

rtl.html

```
<head>
<meta http-equiv="Content-Language" content="en">
<meta http-equiv="Content-Type"
      content="text/html; charset=utf-8">
<title>Unicode BiDirection Override</title>
<style type="text/css">
#s1 { font-family: cursive; font-size: 12pt }
#s2 { unicode-bidi:override; direction: rtl;
      font-family:HebrewUniversal; font-size:20pt }
</style>
</head>
```

*Use **<bdo>** for right-to-left text inserted in a left-to-right text paragraph.*

```
<body>
<p id="s1">Happy New Year</p>
<p id="s2" lang="he">שנה טובה</p>
</body>
```

Text capitalization

The style **text-transform** property can be used to convert the capitalization of text content.

It may be used to transform text into **uppercase** or **lowercase** or it may make the first letter of each word into a capital letter when set as **capitalize**.

This example illustrates each type of transformation:

transform.html

```
<head>
<title>Text Transform</title>
<style type="text/css">
div { border:1px solid silver; padding:5px; margin:5px }
#d1 { text-transform:uppercase; color:red }
#d2 { text-transform:lowercase; color:green }
#d3 { text-transform:capitalize; color:blue }
</style>
</head>

<body>
<div id="d1">This Line is Transformed to Uppercase</div>
<div id="d2">This Line is Transformed to Lowercase</div>
<div id="d3">This Line is Transformed to Capitalize
</div>
</body>
```

Text may not be transformed for content in languages that use other than standard Latin characters.

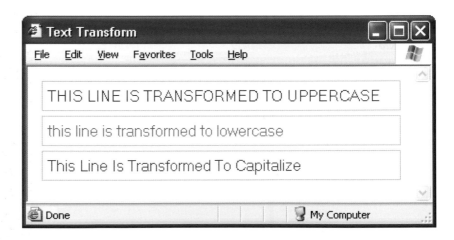

List and table styles

This chapter presents further options for how text lists and content tables may be displayed in a HTML document. There are examples illustrating how their presentation can be influenced with Cascading Style Sheet rules.

Covers

Chapter Fourteen

List style types

The HTML list styles can alternatively be specified by the style **list-style-type** property. This may specify that each list item should be marked as **disc**, **circle**, **square**, **decimal**, **lower-roman**, **upper-roman**, **lower-alpha**, or **upper-alpha**.

The specifications also allow for foreign language list styles to be marked as **hebrew**, **georgian**, **armenian**, **katakana**, **cjk-ideographic** or **hiragana**.

In the event that the specified list style type is not supported the browser will default to the **decimal** numbering style.

With alpha marking most browsers will list the first 26 items with successive lettering then start with AA, BB, etc.

The example below illustrates a simple list specifying the **disc** type of list style to create filled circular bullet points:

liststyle.html

```
<head>
<title>List Style Type</title>
<style type="text/css">
ol { list-style-type:disc; color:red }
</style>
</head>

<body>
<ol>
<li>Pascal Programming</li>
<li>Java Programming</li>
</ol>
</body>
```

Browsers may not support foreign language list style types.

List style position

The position of item markers in a list can be set with the style **list-style-position** property.

This allows the marker to be either **outside** or **inside** the content box containing the list, as seen in this example:

liststylepos.html

```
<head>
<title>List Style Position</title>
<style type="text/css">
ul     { list-style-type:circle }
#list1 { list-style-position:outside; color:red }
#list2 { list-style-position:inside; color:blue }
</style>
</head>

<body>
<ul id="list1"><li>Pascal<br>Programming With Units</li>
         <li>Java<br>Programming With Classes</li></ul>
<ul id="list2"><li>Pascal<br>Programming With Units</li>
         <li>Java<br>Programming With Classes</li> </ul>
</body>
```

Notice that the first style rule sets the marker type for both unordered lists.

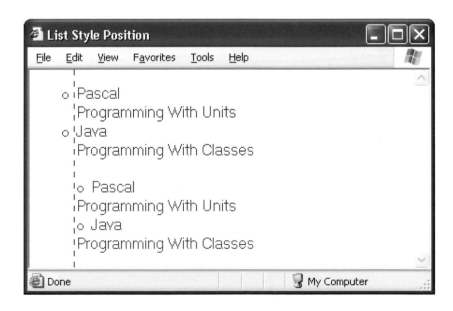

List style image

More creative lists can be made by replacing the standard markers for each item with a custom marker image. The location of the image to be used should be specified with the style **list-style-image** property. It must be assigned inside plain brackets following the term **url**.

The location can be either an absolute address, such as **"http://domain/pic.gif"**, or a relative address like **"pic.gif"**. If the image is unavailable the list uses **decimal** markers.

In the example below the list markers are set as an image with a relative location address in a stylesheet class:

listimg.html

```
<head>
<title>List Style Image</title>
<style type="text/css">
ol.lilguy { list-style-image:url("lilguy.gif") }
</style>
</head>

<body>
<ol class="lilguy">
<li>Pascal<br>Programming With Units</li>
<li>Java<br>Programming With Classes</li>
</ol>
</body>
```

Remember to surround the location address with quotes.

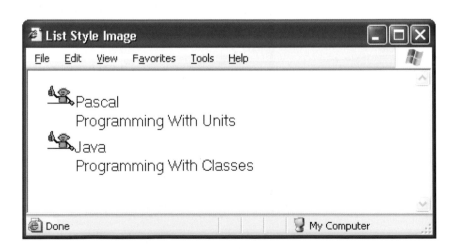

List style shorthand

All list styles can be specified together using the **list-style** property to set the list's type, position and marker image.

The example below uses this shorthand method to specify the list properties for an outer list and a nested list:

listshort.html

```
<head>
<title>List Style Shorthand</title>
<style type="text/css">
#outerlist { list-style:square outside url("star.gif") }
#innerlist { list-style:disc inside url("duke.gif") }
</style>
</head>

<body>
<ul id="outerlist">
<li>Pascal<br>Programming With Units</li>
<li>Java<br>Programming With Classes
    <ul id="innerlist">
    <li>Applets</li>
    <li>Swing Interface</li>
    </ul>
</ul>
</body>
```

Note that a list will be displayed with the specified marker type if the image cannot be found.

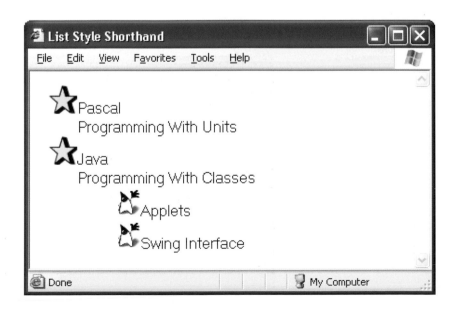

Table caption side

The position of a table caption relative to the table may be specified with the style **caption-side** property. This can set the caption's position at the **top**, **bottom**, **left** or **right** of the table.

In the example below the **caption-side** property positions the caption to the right of the table. The caption is 80 pixels wide, with a left margin of 5 pixels, and is vertically aligned with the bottom of the table:

captionside.html

```
<head>
<title>Caption Side</title>
<style type="text/css">
caption { caption-side:right; margin-left:5px;
          width:80px; vertical-align:bottom;
          color:purple; background-color:yellow;
          font-weight:bold }
td { text-align:center; width:50px; height:50px }
</style>
</head>

<body>
<table cellspacing="3" border="1">
<caption>Descriptive Caption</caption>
<tr> <td>1</td> <td>2</td> <td>3</td> </tr>
<tr> <td>4</td> <td>5</td> <td>6</td> </tr>
</table>
</body>
```

The property *vertical-align* can specify **top**, **middle** or **bottom**.

Browsers that do not support this property will normally position the caption above the table.

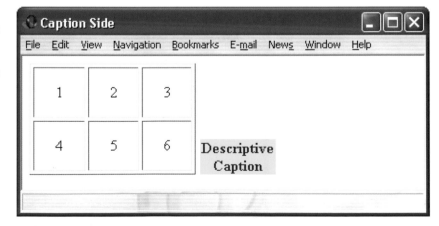

Collapsing table borders

Individual table border styles can be applied to cells, rows and columns with their style **border** property as usual.

Visually this can appear cluttered but the **border-collapse** style property can be set to **collapse** so that only the most prominent border will be displayed.

The example below specifies a single-pixel blue border around each cell but these are collapsed to unite together:

collapse.html

```
<head>
<title>Border-Collapse</title>
<style type="text/css">
table { border-collapse:collapse;
        border:5px double red }
td { border:1px solid blue; padding:1em }
td.dash { border: 5px dashed green }
td.solid { border: 5px solid orange }
</style>
</head>
<body>
<table>
<tr> <td>1</td> <td>2</td> <td>3</td> </tr>
<tr> <td class="dash">4</td><td>5</td>
     <td class="solid">6</td> </tr>
</table>
</body>
```

The overall table border has prominence over other table border styles.

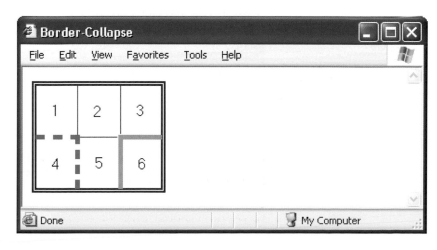

Empty cell borders

Table cells that contain no content may have their borders hidden by setting the style **empty-cell** property to **hide**. This property can be applied to the entire table so that all empty cell borders are hidden.

Note that an empty cell's background will remain visible even when the **empty-cell** property is set to **hide**.

The example below hides the borders of all its empty cells. In order to make cell 4 seem completely invisible its **background-color** is set to **yellow** to match the page background:

emptycell.html

```
<head>
<title>Empty Cells</title>
<style type="text/css">
body { background-color:yellow }
table { text-align:center }
td { border:purple 5px double; background-color:lime }
#cell4 { background-color:yellow }
</style>
</head>

<body>
<table width="150px" cellspacing="3">
<tr> <td>1</td> <td>2</td> <td></td> </tr>
<tr> <td id="cell4"></td> <td>5</td> <td>6</td> </tr>
</table>
</body>
```

If this table had a background color, that would still be visible overall.

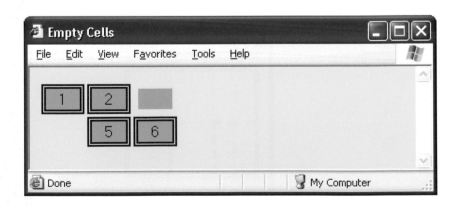

Styling backgrounds

This chapter demonstrates how style sheet techniques may display content backgrounds in a HTML document. Further style rule examples illustrate cursor choice, content clipping and automatic content insertion.

Covers

Chapter Fifteen

Background color

The background color of HTML elements can be specified with the style **background-color** property. Foreground color is normally black by default but can be changed for each element with the style **color** property.

This example illustrates how background and foreground colors may be specified for different elements:

backcolor.html

```
<head>
<title>Background &amp; Foreground Color</title>
<style type="text/css">
body { background-color:white }
h3 { background-color: purple; color:yellow }
p  { background-color: lime }
</style>
</head>
```

It can be useful to set a background to a value of ***transparent***.

```
<body>
<h3>Hiking</h3>
<p>Both Heraklion and Chania have clubs that organize
hiking trips.</p>
<h3>Flora</h3>
<p>Crete is a year-round showcase of flowers and
trees.</p>
</body>
```

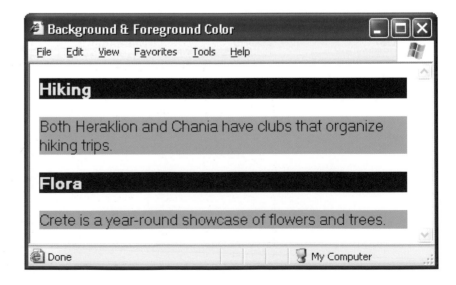

Background image

The background of a HTML element can feature an image using the style **background-image** property. This states the location of an image as an absolute or relative address between brackets and preceded by the term **url**. A background color should also be specified that will display beneath the image. The specified background color will be displayed even when the image is not available and the color will show through any transparent areas of the background image.

Browsers will normally "tile" the image by repeating it both horizontally and vertically across the element background.

This example tiles an image over the document body background and on top of a white background color:

backimage.html

Remember to surround the image address with quotes.

```
<head>
<title>Background Image</title>
<style type="text/css">
body {background-color:white; text-align:center;
      background-image: url("mug.gif") }
p {font-size:36pt; font-style:italic; font-weight:bold }
</style>
</head>

<body>
<p>Coffee<br>Time !</p>
</body>
```

Background repeat

The way a background image is repeated across an element can be set with the style **background-repeat** property. If a **repeat-x** value is specified the image will be repeated in a single horizontal line only. If a **repeat-y** value is specified the image will be repeated in a single vertical line only.

In both cases the sequence starts with the top left corner of the image at the top left corner of the element (x=0, y=0).

This example creates two **<div>** content blocks illustrating horizontally and vertically repeated background images:

backrepeat.html

```
<head>
<title>Background Repeat</title>
<style type="text/css">
body { text-align:center; color:purple;
       font-weight:bold }
div { position:absolute; top:20px; width:160px;
      height:60px; background-image:url("box.gif");
      background-color:yellow }
#d1 { background-repeat: repeat-x; left:30px }
#d2 { background-repeat: repeat-y; left:220px }
</style>
</head>

<body>
<div id="d1"><br>repeat-x</div>
<div id="d2"><br>repeat-y</div>
</body>
```

This example is repeating this single image:

*Use **no-repeat** to stop the background image from repeating.*

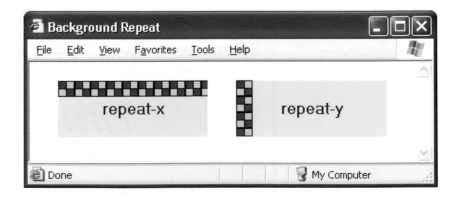

Background position

The position of a background image can be specified using the style **background-position** property to set its top left corner relative to the edges of its containing content box. Position values may be expressed as pixels or percentages or with keywords **top**, **bottom**, **left**, **right** and **center**. Keywords cannot be mixed with pixel or percentage values.

If only one length value is specified it will set the horizontal position of the background image. If two length values are specified the first sets the horizontal position while the second will set the vertical position.

The following example demonstrates the use of keywords and percentages to set the background image positions:

backposition.html

*The **center** keyword used alone centers the background image on both horizontal and vertical axes.*

```
<head>
<title>Background Position</title>
<style type="text/css">
div { position:absolute; top:5px; width:100px;
      height:60px; background-image:url("box.gif");
      background-color:yellow; color:purple }
#d1 { background-position:center;
      background-repeat:no-repeat; left:20px }
#d2 { background-position: 50% 100%;
      background-repeat:no-repeat; left:140px }
</style>
</head>

<body>
<div id="d1">center</div> <div id="d2">50% 100%</div>
</body>
```

*The position of "50% 100%" is equivalent to the same position with keywords **center bottom**.*

Background attachment

Typically background images will scroll along with the document but they can be fixed using the style property called **background-attachment**. Setting this property to **fixed** keeps the **background-image** position constant when the rest of the document scrolls.

This example fixes a horizontally repeated image at a specified distance from the top of the window:

backattach.html

```
<head>
<title>Background Attachment</title>
<style type="text/css">
body { background-attachment:fixed; text-align:center;
       background-position:0% 30%;
       background-repeat:repeat-x;
       background-image:url("box.gif") }
</style>
</head>

<body>
<h1>Heading</h1>
</body>
```

This is useful to ensure that background logos are always visible.

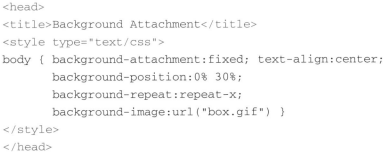

As the normal content scrolls the fixed content remains in a constant position.

Background shorthand

All the background properties can be set together using the style **background** property with this syntax:

```
background: color image repeat position attachment ;
```

Some or all of the above may be specified, and in any order. The valid values are those stated on the previous pages in this chapter for **background-color**, **background-image**, **background-repeat**, **background-position** and **background-attachment**.

In the example below the **<div>** element background repeats a fixed image across the bottom of its content box:

backshort.html

```
<head>
<title>Background Shorthand</title>
<style type="text/css">
body { text-align:center; font:14pt cursive black }
div { width:90%; height:70px; border:3px double black }
#d1 { background:white url("mug.gif") bottom
      repeat-x fixed }
</style>
</head>

<body>
<div id="d1">Coffee Time !</div>
</body>
```

Specify font sizes to absolutely control text in content boxes.

Visibility

Content boxes may be hidden by setting the style **visibility** property to **hidden** or revealed when it is set to **visible**. This is most useful with scripts to toggle the visibility of content in response to an event triggered by the user.

The example below creates two content boxes at the same XY position but with different Z-index values.

The top layer is initially hidden but may be revealed when the user places the cursor over the third content box:

visibility.html

```
<head>
<title>Visibility</title>
<style type="text/css">
#d1,#d2,#d3 { position:absolute; top:20px;
                left:20px; width:100px }
#d2 { z-index:10; visibility:hidden;
      background-color:red; color:white }
#d3 { top:40px }
</style>
</head>

<body>
<div id="d1">Action is OFF</div>
<div id="d2">Action is ON</div>
<div id="d3" onmouseover="d2.style.visibility='visible'"
             onmouseout="d2.style.visibility='hidden'">
Roll pointer over here to turn on.</div>
</body>
```

Notice how the stylesheet can apply style rules to several tags at once.

Cursors

The type of cursor to be displayed over elements can be specified with the style **cursor** property.

Common valid pointer values include **default**, **crosshair**, **move**, **text**, **wait**, and **help** as seen in the table below:

Name	Cursor	Pointer Type
default		Browser's default cursor
pointer		Hand pointer indicating a link
crosshair		Pinpoint selector
move		Selection relocator
text		Text highlighter
wait		Program busy indicator
help		Help available indicator
resize		Edge indicator
url		Specify remote cursor address

The browser will determine the precise appearance of each cursor.

The resize cursor is a pointer that indicates a direction and can be set as **n-resize**, **s-resize**, **w-resize**, **e-resize**, **ne-resize**, **nw-resize**, **se-resize**, or **sw-resize** – the table above shows the **e-resize** cursor.

A custom cursor can be used by specifying the location of a cursor image with the term **url:**. For instance:

```
cursor:url("http://domain/folder/special.cur");
```

The location is stated as either a relative or absolute address between quotes and inside brackets after the **url:** term.

Hyperlink colors

Anchor **<a>** tags have the "pseudo-classes" listed in the table below which are useful to influence the appearance of their content. A stylesheet may set different property values for each pseudo-class to indicate the hyperlink's state to the user. The ensuing example sets color and font properties for each state.

Name	Description
:link	The default state of an un-visited hyperlink
:hover	A hyperlink that has the cursor over it
:active	A hyperlink that is being clicked by the user
:visited	The default state of a visited hyperlink

links.html

```
<head>
<title>Link Colors</title>
<style type="text/css">
a { font-size:18pt }
a:link    { color:red; font-style:normal }
a:hover   { color:fuchsia; font-weight:bold }
a:active  { color:green; font-weight:bold }
a:visited { color:blue; font-style:italic }
</style>
</head>

<body> <p>    <a href="x.html">Link 1</a>
               <a href="y.html">Link 2</a>
               <a href="z.html">Link 3</a>      </p>
</body>
```

Keep to one font style for all states to avoid the content "jumping" to accommodate changing styles.

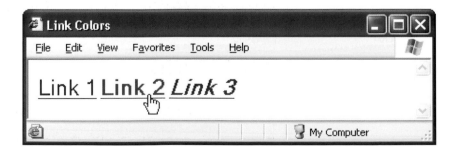

Additional content

Style sheets may automatically insert content into HTML elements with the "pseudo-elements" listed in the table below. The example uses pseudo-elements to add three dots after every **\<h3\>** heading, emphasize the first letter of each paragraph and end each paragraph with an exclamation mark.

Name	Description
:before	The space immediately before element content
:after	The space immediately after element content
:first-letter	The first letter of a \<p\> element
:first-line	The first line of a \<p\> element

added.html

```
<head>
<title>Additional Content</title>
<style type="text/css">
p { font-family:cursive }
h3:after { content:"..."; color:blue }
p:first-letter { font-size:larger; color:red }
p:after { content:" !"; color:green }
</style>
</head>
```

Pseudo-elements may not be fully implemented in all browsers.

```
<body>
<h3>And Finally</h3>
<p>HTML is Fantastic Fun in easy steps</p>
</body>
```

What next?

This book will, hopefully, have provided you with a great introduction to HTML with Cascading Style Sheets for the creation of exciting visual content.

Catering for future browser devices, style sheets properties already exist to control aural content, as listed in this table:

Property Type	Property Names
Volume	volume
Pause	pause, pause-before, pause-after
Cue	cue, cue-before, cue-after
Mixing	play-during
Spatial	azimuth, elevation
Voice	voice, voice-family, speech, speech-rate, pitch, pitch-range, stress, richness
Speak	speak, speak-header, speak-pronunciation, speak-numeral

Longer term plans for Internet content are increasingly focusing on the Extensible Hypertext Markup Language (XHTML).

This is like a stricter version of HTML that adds the ability to create your own tags and has other features that are well suited to data handling.

For the very latest developments in HTML and XHTML refer to the W3C Web site at **http://www.w3c.org**.

The countless millions of HTML documents that are in current existence ensure that implementation of newer specifications must be a gradual building process.

This means that HTML documents created with the strict HTML standard used throughout this book will remain valid for the foreseeable future – happy coding!

Index

M

N

O

P

Q tag   33
QuickTime media player   98
Quotes   33

Radio buttons   115
Readonly attribute   117
Real media player   99
Recommendations   18
Rect type   86
Refresh type   22
Rel attribute   28
Relative address   11
Relative positioning   145
Reset buttons   119
Revisions   18
RGB colors   50
Right-to-left languages   164–165
Rows   64
    Adding   67
    Attribute   104, 124
    Spanning   68
Rowspan attribute   68
Rules attribute   73

Samp tag   40
Scheme attribute   25
Script tag   26
Scrolling attribute   106
Search engines   24
Select tag   125
Selected attribute   126

Selection menu   126
Semi-colon   46
Shape attribute   86
Simple forms   110
Single-line comments   15
Size attribute   112
Small tag   36
Sound   96
Spaces   15
Span attribute   74
Span tag   54
Square type   57
Src attribute   88, 121
Src type   98
Strict DTD   13
Strong tag   35
Structure   14
Style
    Attribute   44, 65
    Tag   27
Stylesheet   18, 27, 46
Styling tags   47
Sub tag   38
Sub-folder   11
Submit buttons   120–121
Subscript   38
Summary attribute   76
Sup tag   38
Superscript   38

Tabindex attribute   125
Table
    Borders   173
    Captions   172
    Columns   74
    Frame   73
    Positioning   66
    Rules   73
    Simple   64
    Summary   76
    Tag   64
Tabs   15
Tag attributes   44–45
Tags   8
Target attribute   107
Tbody tag   70
Td tag   64